BLUEPRINT

Revised Edition

High Point Church
Madison, WI

BLUEPRINT

A GOSPEL FOUNDATION FOR BUILDING AN
UNCLUTTERED AND UNSTUCK CHURCH

Nicola Gibson

Revised Edition

All Scripture quotations, unless otherwise indicated, are from: *The Holy Bible, New International Version®*. Copyright © 1973, 1978, 1984 by International Bible Society. Used by permission of International Bible Society.

Bold text within Scripture quotations indicate emphasis added.

Find resources for BLUEPRINT at *hpcmadison.com/blueprint*.

Developmental and Lead Editor: Hannah Sevedge
Production and Project Editor: Lisa Dahlager
Copy-editors: Lindsay Armstrong, Kate Beecken, Jean Collins, Hannah Donor *(also compiled edits)*, Cristy Jefson, Andrea Mellinger, Antonio Tang.
Cover design and book graphics: Daniel Hoopes

Fonts downloaded for use in this book: Ostrich Sans by Tyler Finck *(tylerfinck.com)* downloaded at *fontsquirrel.com*. Code and Code Pro Demo by Fontfabric *(fontfabric.com)* downloaded from *dafont.com* and *myfonts.com*. Sinkin Sans by K-Type *(k-type.com)* downloaded at *fontsquirrel.com*.

Printed by CreateSpace in the United States of America

THANK YOU

Like most useful endeavors the production of the Blueprint series is the accomplishment of diverse and very committed people. When we began I expected to essentially republish the RENEW campaign guide, a book I published in 2010. But, as I attempted to adjust that book to what we are trying to accomplish in High Point Church, I found myself rewriting at every turn. I suspect I have rewritten somewhere between 65-80% of the book. This of course made the production of *Blueprint* far more arduous than any of us expected—and hopefully more useful. My two most tireless co-laborers have no doubt been Lisa Dahlager and Hannah Sevedge, the latter editing from West Africa and then Southern Italy. Hannah perhaps spent as much time editing this text as I have re-written it all while knowing she will not be in the United States to participate in the series. It says much about her love for Christ and the little flock at High Point.

The text has been read and reread by many competent editors: Lindsay Armstrong, Kate Beecken, Jean Collins, Hannah Donor, Cristy Jefson, Andrea Mellinger and Antonio Tang. Many other small contributions were made by people who are left unnamed. Dan Hoopes was the point artist for much of our imaging. Andrea Mellinger both edited text and was the point person project managing the execution of the campaign itself among the staff departments. One last person who made as many sacrifices for this project as anyone is my wife Alexi. The ministry of mothering in my times of intensified ministry and parental absence is one she bears with great understanding and hope. She is a great joy to me and a vigorous nurturer of our little brood.

Yet for all this, none of the above servants would wish to receive thanks. All the motivating dedication that was orchestrated in the collaboration of this book and series is dedicated to the good name of Christ and for the spiritual rooting and strengthening of his flock, the church. To all who helped in production of the resources, or later in the execution of the campaign, it was a pleasure to work with all of you. And now, I share all of your hopes, that God would use all of our labors for his glory and his redemptive purposes.

This book is dedicated to the present and future people of the High Point flock. That they may be free to stand on the peace and purity of the Gospel foundation, and in it, to find hopeful humility and the boldness of lions.

Or to put it as the apostle Paul did:

> *"Therefore, my dear brothers and sisters, stand firm. Let nothing move you. Always give yourselves fully to the work of the Lord, because you know that your labor in the Lord is not in vain."*
>
> 1 Corinthians 15:58

CONTENTS

PREFACE

Most people know what a blueprint is. It is a fairly detailed and accurate plan of a structure that shows those details superimposed onto the whole. When you look at a blueprint, you can see where everything goes in relation and proportion to everything else, as well as how each part contributes to the whole. Although a blueprint is still fairly complicated, it drastically simplifies something much more complex, something that would otherwise be very challenging for us to get our minds around. It's useful because it simplifies things while retaining the necessary detail and integrity of the plan. It allows you to understand the building task and to get excited about the ultimate goal instead of being overwhelmed by it.

Christian faith and life can often seem anything but clear and simple. Modern people often feel like their lives, minds and emotions are stuck and cluttered. We feel like we aren't making progress in our character and our emotions are taxed and fluctuating. Our minds sound like a tree full of screaming monkeys. There's no peace and no focus. Yet, when we look to Jesus, the Bible and the Christian message, the answers there feel either too simplistic or too complex to be of real help. It seems like either a crayon drawing or a mystifyingly overcomplicated schematic. It just doesn't hit the sweet spot of a blueprint.

Our goal for this book and experience is to simplify and clarify how we can know God and grow spiritually in a way that loses its paralyzing complexity while retaining the Gospel's full integrity. It is our intention that by going through it together, it will help us love God, know him better and stay on mission together. This will create real rest and help us grow our passions, form our character, foster unity and build humility. We want to understand the elementary truths needed to grow in Christ while becoming united around a plan for how to do ministry together in the local church, in our city and in our world.

This book is organized around the interconnection of relationships, understanding and action, or hopefully more memorably: Connect, Grow and Serve. Jesus once said that we should love God with all our heart, mind and strength, and that we should love others as ourselves. Love, toward God or others, assumes some kind of relationship. So *connecting* is a necessary component of real spiritual life.

Yet, how we should feel, what we should believe and what we should do have to have a relationship to the truth. Jesus claimed that he came to reveal the truth, that he taught only the truth, that he is the truth and that the truth would set us free. Consequently, we need to *grow* in our knowledge of the truth. To do this, we need to grow both in understanding the central concepts embodied in Christ's life, death and resurrection (what we call "the Gospel") and in our knowledge of the entirety of God's written revelation, the Bible.

Lastly, Jesus is a person of action. His love is a vigorous and active love, characterized by *serving* humanity in the most sacrificial and powerful way. Jesus said he "did not come to be served, but to serve, and to give his life as a ransom for many" (Mark 10:45). In that same passage, he taught all of his followers that we are to be servants too. Everyone who loves Jesus loves, learns and does. They connect. They grow. They serve.

The following readings are designed to support the concepts I believe are the most important for every Christian to know personally and for every church to embody corporately. It is a blueprint for anyone who does not really know what Christian faith is about, or who realizes that their perceptions might be wrong. Misperceptions cause us to feel stuck or make us desperate for any possible answer, leading to clutter. Picture two hikers, one who doesn't know which trail to take (stuck), and the other wearing a backpack so full of non-essential weight that he can't make the climb (cluttered). *Blueprint* is for both. It is designed to get us moving spiritually in the right direction and to free us of the confusion and stress of non-essential distractions. It is designed to help us build our lives on a Gospel foundation, allowing us to have an uncluttered and unstuck life.

We were meant to live lives that glorify God, that show people his real greatness so they can trust and enjoy him forever, too. It's true that Jesus said loving and enjoying God by following him would often feel like dying, that we'd have to deny ourselves and take up our cross to follow him (Luke 9:23). Yet he also said that serving him was an easy and light burden, and that in him, our souls would find rest (Matthew 11:29-30). This is no contradiction. It is the heart of the divine genius of biblical Christian faith. Find the place where Jesus brings those two things together, and you will find a life and purpose you never thought possible.

CONNECT

WEEK 1
CONNECT
WITH GOD

These first two weeks are about connecting. They are about embracing the relationships for which God created us and in which he builds our understanding and character, but they aren't just task-oriented relationships. They are also relationships of care, provision and enjoyment. God is a shepherd, and he calls his people his "flock." We are the sort of creatures that were made to care and be cared for; we were made for community. We were designed to love, be loved and want love.

No matter what our personality types or vocational skills, we were made to relate, first to God and then to everything else. Just as we were made to let God bring out our creative potential, he gave us the work of bringing the potential out of his creation (Genesis 1:28). It's no wonder that in the first two chapters of the Bible, God had already invented a place to commune with him, as well as two complimentary genders, families and work. All of these are forms of right connectedness, including the structural components of provision and protection (traditionally masculine) and the organic components of nurture and beauty (traditionally feminine).

Everything and everyone are inherently related to our creator and to all of creation. It is this connection, this relationship, that we have broken, and that God is setting right again through Christ.

On every page of the Bible, God shows himself to be a personal being. His ultimate revelation of himself was becoming visible as a human person, Jesus the Savior. God reveals himself as a person, not merely as an energy, an ultimate reality or a set of principles.

Once we see that this is the biblical portrayal of God, whatever we do or think in relationship to this God is by definition relating and connecting, because that is what you do with a person. And so, in the clearest possible terms, Christian faith must be a relationship. If God is a person, and if we relate to each other in any way, then what we have is, by definition, a relationship, and all relationships begin with and are fed by connection.

From this basic realization we say things like, "Christianity is a relationship, not a religion," or ask, "Do you have a relationship with God?" Although this relationship will be significantly different than all our other relationships in ways that will both amaze you and frustrate you, it is still, first and foremost, a relationship. Your faith can never be what God intends for it to be until it is explicitly relational. Once we realize this basic truth, much of the rest falls into place with beautiful simplicity.

WEEK 1
CONNECT
WITH GOD

SERMON NOTES

CONNECT
WITH GOD

SMALL GROUP
DISCUSSION QUESTIONS

WATCH THE SMALL GROUP VIDEO

1. What do you mean when you say you "have a relationship with God"?

2. How does one have "a relationship with God"?

3. In the reading from Day 2 it talks about God's love as holy love and it also discusses the "depravity" of our human condition. What realizations or questions emerged from that section?

4. Discuss the questions from the end of the readings on Day 2 on page 31 and Day 3 on page 37.

5. In the reading from Day 4, there is a figure containing the four effects of conversion.
   a. Which do you usually think about and which do you tend to forget about?
   b. How should each affect how you think about who you are?

DAY 1

What is a "Relationship with God?"

Christians often talk about having a "relationship with God" or "knowing Christ." While it is part of the Christian jargon, this language often confuses people who are trying to figure Jesus out. But here's a dirty little secret: Many Christians aren't really sure what they mean by it either. The first five days of this study are focused on what it means to connect with, or have a relationship with, God.

On the one hand, the idea of "connecting with God" or having a "relationship with God" should seem logical. What do we call it when two persons relate to each other? We call it a relationship. Rationally, then, if God exists and relates to us (no matter what the relating consists of), then the simple truth is that we have a relationship, no matter how incomprehensibly big or complicated God is.

On the other hand, however, saying we can "have a relationship with God" may feel very unrealistic. We might wonder how we are supposed to have a relationship with someone in a way that's completely different from how we relate to everyone else. How do you have a relationship with someone you can't see or feel and who never talks to you "like a normal person"? Even if you compare it to a relationship between a person and a lesser consciousness, like a dog, the concept tends to get more confusing (and insulting) rather than clearer.

This is why Christian faith starts not with our emotional or rational sentiments but instead with God's acts of speaking and showing himself to us, especially through Jesus. One of Jesus' best summaries is this one:

> After Jesus said this, he looked toward heaven and prayed: "Father, the time has come. Glorify your Son, that your Son may glorify you. ²For you granted him

authority over all people that he might give eternal life to all those you have given him. ³Now this is eternal life: that they may know you, the only true God, and Jesus Christ, whom you have sent."

John 17:1-3

We're not accustomed to that language, but it's pretty clear. To glorify something means to show its inherent character and value, and to take its real meaning and beauty and put it on display for others to see, enjoy and respond to. Jesus wants us to see something about him so that we can see something about the Father. Jesus said that the Father has given him all authority so that we could have eternal life. Now is eternal life just life that keeps on going and doesn't end? No. The essence of eternal life is that it is an eternal *relatedness to God.* Jesus goes out of his way to make this clear in verse three. Knowing God by knowing Jesus is not just the source, but the heart, of eternal life.

> Christian faith starts not with our emotional or rational sentiments, but instead with God's acts of speaking and showing himself to us, especially through Jesus.

In this passage, Jesus is just restating what God said before his coming and pointing us to God's end game for all of creation, as revealed in the last chapters of the Bible. Six hundred years before Jesus came, the prophet Jeremiah said that there was going to be a "new covenant," a new way God would relate with people. Jeremiah said one of the results of it would be that, "They will be my people and I will be their God" (Revelation 21:3). That is, people would have a restored *relationship* with God.

In the second-to-last chapter of the Bible, an angel announces the significance of the "new heavens and the new earth," which people usually call "heaven." Everything is remade, but the thing that is most different about this new version is that God and his creation are *together.* John says in Revelation 21:3, "And I heard a loud voice from the throne saying, 'Now the dwelling of God is with men, and he will live with them. They will be his people, and God himself will be with them and be their God.'" The relationship that was broken by sin is restored.

It is also possible to see God's relational intention in all the ways Jesus talks to his followers. He uses a whole string of relational categories to talk about those who believe in him. They are his friends, his servants, his bride, his heirs, his sons and daughters, his little flock and little chicks that need care, and so on. When he talks about his presence through the Holy Spirit in John 14:17-18, he says, "I will not leave you as orphans," and the Holy Spirit will be *with* you" and "*in* you." These categories are not just relational but are the most intimate relational categories we have.

When the Bible points to judgment, it is often spoken of not merely in legal terms but in terms of betrayal and even adultery, which are intensely relational categories. In the first chapters of the Bible, God crowns his created world with beings endowed with a capacity to know him and act for him (made in his image). He created two genders for each other and invented marriage between them, and it is precisely this marriage relationship that God uses as the best picture of our eternal relationship with himself (Ephesians 5:22-33; Malachi 2:11-16).

Even God's moral statements assume his relational intention. What does immorality do to this intention? Immorality is in most cases anti-social or anti-relational behavior. It destroys our relationships with people, with the created world in which God put us and with the creator to whom everything belongs.

Even direct moral commandments, the part of the Bible people tend to like the least, are rooted in relationship. They're designed to make possible a long-term, stable and meaningful relationship between God, ourselves and all of creation. This produces a relational state that the Bible's Old Testament calls "shalom," defined as a peaceful state of justice in which all things are in right relationship with each other.[1] It is the world the way it was created, should be, is not and will be again.

Shalom is the type of relationship God is after; it is the redemption Jesus came to re-create. So why is relating to God so difficult? Well, every relationship has at least three components: the two persons doing the relating and the dynamic of the relationship itself. Jesus came to help us with all three. He came to reveal God, the person we are to relate to. He came to tell us the truth about ourselves, a message we generally don't want to hear. He also came to provide the solution for the dynamic between us, which we'll talk more about more in the upcoming readings.

---

1 "In the Bible shalom means universal flourishing, wholeness, and delight—a rich state of affairs in which natural needs are satisfied and natural gifts fruitfully employed, a state of affairs that inspires joyful wonder as its Creator and Savior opens doors and welcomes the creatures in whom he delights. Shalom, in other words, is the way things ought to be." Cornelius Plantinga, Jr., *A Breviary of Sin: Not the Way It's Supposed to Be* (Grand Rapids, MI: Eerdmans Publishing Co., 1995).

DAY 2

The Three Components of a Relationship

To recap from yesterday, all relationships have three main components: the two persons doing the relating and the dynamic of the relationship. When it comes to relating to God, we have to know something about God, ourselves and the dynamic between us. We'll look at the first two components in this reading and explore the third in day three.

COMPONENT 1: GOD'S NATURE AND CHARACTER

Before we start to answer the question of what God is like, we need to know if we *can* even know what God is like. Can we even talk about this? Christian faith is founded on the notion that we could not know God if he didn't speak and show himself. He is, though, a self-revealing God. He has revealed himself through his interaction with the Jewish people and the Church, through what is written down for us in the Bible, and most profoundly through the life, death and resurrection of Jesus. We can know what God is like because he wants to be known, and because he is by nature relational. So what does he want us to know about himself?

The first and most central concept God reveals about himself is what the Bible calls his holiness. That's not a very popular concept today. Most people think that the central concept should be love; it should be something more pleasant or obvious than holiness. What does that word even mean? Holiness refers to at least three things:

1. **Greatness** (sometimes "majesty"): God is completely and totally superior in beauty and grandeur to everything to which you can compare him. Only God deserves the literal description of "awesome."

2. **Uniqueness**: There is nothing and no one like God either in quantity or quality. There are things similar to

God[1], but ultimately they cannot compare.

3. **Moral purity and stability**: God always believes and holds to the right thing for the right reason, in the right way and for the right duration. He does so in perfect proportion and intensity.

You might still ask, "But what about love?" Well the nature of God's love (as with the rest of his attributes) doesn't make sense without his holiness. God's love is a love like we've never imagined (greatness). It is of a quantity and quality that we have never experienced and to which we ultimately cannot compare ourselves (uniqueness). But his love is also morally serious (pure and stable). Because he loves all things the right way—with the right motives and proportion—his love is never insecure, manipulated, self-indulgent, narcissistic, codependent, enabling or dishonest. Our love may exhibit these things and, frankly, many of us in our less noble moments *wish* his love would be more like ours. But his love isn't like ours. He is none of these things. God loves us with holiness. God's love is holy.

As another example, God's holiness also defines his justice. God doesn't just love *us* perfectly. His perfect love includes everything that is good, true and beautiful. He also perfectly loves the proper *interrelationship* of all things. He loves *shalom*. That is, he not only loves us, but he also loves everything that we've screwed up, rejected, rebelled against and been dismissive about.

God's justice is holy. God designed us to bring the creative potential out of his world and to relate to himself and to others in justice and truth.[2] That's not exactly what we've done, not by a long shot. We haven't done it in our relationship with God. We haven't done it in our relationship with

---

1 Take graciousness for example. God is gracious and humans can be gracious. However, we do not fully understand or participate in the way God is gracious or the amount God is gracious. As it says in Isaiah 55:8, "'My thoughts are not your thoughts, neither are your ways my ways,' declares the Lord."

2 This comes from combining the command of God in the law (found in the books of Genesis, Exodus, Leviticus, Numbers and Deuteronomy) and the creation mandate in Genesis 1:28. Both of these are realized and fulfilled in the new covenant of Christ.

creation. We certainly haven't done it in our relationship with the rest of humanity. Because God loves justice perfectly, our relationship with him has become lopsided. We have pitted his holy love and holy justice against each other, and this has produced a perfectly just response in its proper proportion: He's infuriated.[3]

God has revealed himself as a God of holy love and holy justice. Until we realize and fully embrace both proper polarities and recognize the cosmic offense we have created by pitting them against each other, we can never understand who we are relating *to*, who we are relating *as* and how we might be brought back together through the meeting of God's holy love and justice in the life, death and resurrection of Jesus.

COMPONENT 2: HUMAN NATURE AND THE HUMAN CONDITION

The prevailing assumption about human nature in our time and culture is that we are middle-ground creatures. We're "pretty good" as people and "basically good" as a species. But that is not the way things are supposed to be according to Jesus. We are both infinitely greater and infinitely worse. We are more valuable than we ever dared hope and more broken and wicked than we feared.

Our Nature: The Divine Image

From its first page, the Bible claims that our potential and our value are extraordinary. This is rooted in being created "in the image of God" (affirmed in Genesis 1:26-27, 5:3, 9:6; 1 Corinthians 11:7; Colossians 3:10; James 3:9). Our nature is the most foundational and unchangeable part of our existence and being. One of the most terrifying and amazing realities of being created in God's image is that our significance is not in our behavior, circumstances, genetics or accomplishments, but rather our worth is in our human

---

3 Sorry if you don't like that word. But the word angry is too vague and general. Saying God is infuriated is the same as saying God has wrath. The word "wrath" is used more than 190 times in Scripture. It refers to God's passionate, proportionate and appropriate response of anger to sin. Deuteronomy 4:24 and Hebrews 12:29 say that God is a "consuming fire" in his wrath, which literally means to be infuriated.

nature.

Because our significance is in our created nature, it is completely stable and entirely universal in all people in equal measure. This is one of the reasons why everyone can be saved and why Jesus died for the whole world. It is the reason the Bible says that to mock the poor is to mock your Maker (Proverbs 17:5). It is also the reason there is an eternal heaven and hell. We cannot *not* be of eternal consequence because of what we are by nature: eternal beings in the divine image. We're going to look at two important implications of this.

First, this means that we are of incredible value and significance. We are valuable because our Maker values us, not because we can claim certain things to be true about ourselves in terms of our culture, socio-economic status, ethnicity, gender, skills, etc. Our significance includes our moral significance and responsibility. The significance of our nature can be the source of our greatest joy, identity, meaning and security, but it can also be the source of our greatest problem. We'll talk more about that in a minute.

Second, our status as eternal beings means that our inherent value and significance is indissoluble and inoperable. It cannot be removed. His image is inextricable, so your life can't be meaningless, no matter how you think or feel about it. You are incredibly and objectively significant and valuable even if you act in the most degenerate way possible or devalue yourself in the most extreme ways. Being made in God's image wasn't your choice; it was his. You can deny your identity and significance, but you can't change it. We are created in his image and repurchased by his death whether we like it or not. It is true whether we receive it as the best possible news or reject it completely.

Our Condition: The Depraved Condition

The second important thing to know about humanity is our depravity. I use the word depravity because it is more nuanced and precise than "sinful" or "flesh," two words that are in the Bible but are often misunderstood. Depravity is a *condition*, not an act or a nature. You don't do depravity. You ARE depraved. A condition can be a huge part of you, but you would still be you if it were gone. You might not be able to get rid of ADHD or rheumatoid arthritis, but your attitude would be confused if you "couldn't imagine being you" without it. Lose a condition, and you are still yourself. Lose your nature, and you are no longer you. God's image is in our nature. It is who we are. Depravity is a condition that twists our nature and influences our actions.

WHAT DOES DEPRAVITY MEAN?

Depravity is a holistic condition and disposition through which we take our purpose, potential, significance and capacities as bearers of the image of God and re-task them for a purpose opposed to that for which they were originally given. Furthermore, and most seriously for our relationship with God, it is possible because of our God-given independence. Our capacity to independently embrace his holy love and justice is also the capacity to attempt to offend and thwart them.

This is the tragedy and villainy of our depravity. We seek to remake creation to our own selfish liking as if it was from us and for us.[4] We use our power to define salvation and "the good life" for ourselves, all in rebellion against the God who made us in his image.

Cooperating with our depraved condition is rebellion, the most anti-relational act in the universe. In this way, we have not only damaged our relationship with God, but we have damaged every relationship within creation. In our efforts to be our own gods, we make ourselves:

1. **Withered**: Cut off from our source of life.

2. **Broken**: Unable to fulfill our true purpose.

3. **Morally Degenerate**: Smothered by our sin as if by a prolific weed or an aggressive disease.

4. **Trapped**: Stuck in a continuous cycle of willfully acting

---

4   This is what the Bible calls "idolatry"—making "gods" for ourselves, thinking we can remake reality the way we like it.

out our depravity.

5. **Deserving judgment**: Rightfully subject to penalty for misusing God's creation.

How do enemies with such a bitter split come back together? This is the rift Jesus came to close, the slavery he came to liberate. It is the delusion he came to dissipate and the loneliness to which he offers companionship. He has come to destroy our depraved condition while rescuing the very ones whose nature bears his unshakable image.

What can renew this relationship and bring back shalom? What could possibly make things right?

QUESTIONS TO THINK ABOUT

1. Is holiness the first and central attribute of God when you think about him? If not, what do you think of instead? How do you respond differently to thinking about God's "holy love" rather than just "God's love"?

2. Give an example of the relationship between God's holiness and another of his attributes (like justice, wisdom or power). How do you think these attributes might result in different actions if they were not defined by and did not stem from his holiness?

3. Being made in God's image has a lot of gravity to it. How is it more than just a feel good, dignifying idea?

4. In what ways do you feel big enough and small enough to really accept our real identity?

5. When you think about God's image being part of your nature and depravity being a condition that you can still be yourself without, how does that change your outlook on what it means to be human? What does this mean for us when we, talking about our sin, say things like, "Well, that's just part of who I am" or "Can't you just accept me for me?"

DAY 3

Jesus and the Renewed Relationship

In Day 1, you read in John 17 that Jesus said he had come to give eternal life to people, the result of which would be that they would know God and have a relationship with him. Do you remember how the chapter started? It started with this phrase: "The time has come." You wouldn't know this without reading the rest of John's gospel, but John 17 comes directly before Christ's sufferings. When Jesus says, "The time has come," he is referring to his crucifixion, death and resurrection. Somehow the eternal living relationship Jesus gives comes through this great act.

However, Jesus said two things that have to be held together in what is called Christian conversion. To renew the relationship for which we were created so that we can really connect with him, God does something himself and requires something of us. The only thing God demands from us to restore our relationship is sometimes called "repentance and faith."

In the Bible at the very beginning of Mark's gospel, Jesus starts his ministry with these words: "'The time has come,' he said, 'The kingdom of God is near. Repent and believe the good news!'" (Mark 1:15). See that phrase again? "The time has come." In this case, Jesus is not referring to his actions, but to ours. He gives the only biblical condition of receiving a restored relationship with God: "Repent and believe the good news." Repentance means turning around and changing your mind. It is essentially to admit that what you were thinking and where you were going were wrong. Repentance is to believe that it wasn't just wrong in that you are *mistaken*; it was wrong in the sense that you are *guilty*.

"Believing the good news," or having faith, means to do the opposite positive action: to admit that Jesus is right. It is to put the full weight of your trust in what Jesus calls "the good news," which is the literal meaning of the word "gospel."

That is, to restore our relationship with God, he does not require an *action* so much as an *apology*. Repentance is to admit that we did something terribly wrong, to recognize fully and openly that it was wrong and to turn to go in another direction. Faith is to admit that this new direction starts by trusting in the message of the good news. In some ways, repentance and faith are a real and meaningful apology with a pledge of good faith.

When you think about it, this is the only thing an offended person or victim can't do to restore a relationship. If someone does something terrible to you or to someone else, you can bring the people together and you can pay for restitution yourself, but you can't make the perpetrator really apologize from the heart. That is the only thing God won't do.[1] He has done everything else.

Sometimes, particularly with children, we act as though the one making the apology is the one doing all the hard work. This is because it takes parents much more work to get one naughty kid to apologize than to get the other kid to say, "It's okay." But it is the *forgiver* who pays the real cost. It is the offended one who is really doing the hard work. The relationship is restored at the cost of the one forgiving, not the one apologizing. To apologize doesn't earn us anything or take away our guilt. What it does do, if the repentance and faith are sincere, is reopen the relationship. It makes forgiveness receivable. It is an enabler of reconciliation. Still, although the recognition, apology and pledge of good faith are necessary to truly restore a relationship, they are not the actual work of restoration. Jesus had an interaction

---

1   If God won't do it, and if he is as loving and initiating as he is in the rest of redemption, he probably isn't doing it because he shouldn't do it. It either would be to change his character or to destroy something in the fabric of justice in reconciliation and forgiveness. The latter makes sense if you think of the times you've tried to unilaterally forgive someone who is unapologetic. The offense isn't really gone. Trust isn't really restored. The deep heartfelt connection that comes from real restoration doesn't happen. You don't feel closer than ever like many people often feel after a shared, heartfelt reconciliation.

in the book of John that should clear this up pretty well.

READ JOHN 3:1-17

There are probably a couple of things in that passage that are a little confusing. However, the most confusing point for the average modern reader is precisely the point at which Jesus seeks to make everything totally clear. In John 3:14-15, Jesus says, "Just as Moses lifted up the snake in the desert, so the Son of Man must be lifted up, that everyone who believes in him may have eternal life." "Son of Man" is a reference to Jesus himself. Being "lifted up" points both forward to Jesus being lifted up on a cross where everybody can see him, and also points back to a biblical story hardly anyone remembers today. But Nicodemus, the Jewish teacher Jesus is talking to, would definitely know immediately what Jesus meant.

The story is found in Numbers, the fourth book of the Bible. In Numbers 21:4-9 (I'd recommend stopping and going to read that passage right now) God sent a plague of poisonous snakes among the complaining people. They begged God for a remedy to his own judgment, and God told Moses to make a bronze snake.[2] If they were bitten and they simply looked at the crude metal snake, they would live. Period. They simply had to believe God to the point of the very simplest act of obedience, and God would do the impossible for them. If they refused, they would die. Jesus is arguing that the dynamic of coming into a relationship with God is exactly the same in this story about a bronze snake as in his own death and resurrection for us.

God requires repentance and faith. We have to admit that we are wrong and he is right, but that admission has absolutely no power to save or change us. Think about it: What relationship is there between being bitten by a deadly

---

2   Also like Jesus' death and resurrection, God doesn't back down on his judgment, but gives a remedy to survive his own judgment on the people. He offers them a remedy from himself, showing both his commitment to his own character and being (the judgment is just and not a mistake) and his love for the people who deserve the snakes (his holy love in the form of merciful, compassionate provision).

snake and looking at a snake made out of bronze that some-body put on a pole? Looking at a bronze snake doesn't break down venom in the human bloodstream. If God wanted to heal people who had been bitten, why require some bronze snake? Why not just heal them?

It may seem like an odd episode, but there can be no clearer illustration of God's absolute requirement for redemption, or of how functionally insignificant our contribution is. He requires a possible and plain faith in order for him to provide a completely impossible and astounding rescue. The ancient Israelites simply had to believe and follow instructions that could not have been clearer or simpler. They just had to look at something that was in plain view, and that is precisely the point.

God's demand is simply that human beings acknowledge the truth. The Israelites had to acknowledge that they were bitten because they were guilty and that they were dying because of it. They had to acknowledge that they had no option for rescue other than the one God provided. Jesus says in effect, "The cross is just like that." We have to admit that we are dying because we're guilty, and we're guilty because we're depraved and sinful. When we acknowledge it,

> There can be no clearer illustration of God's absolute requirement for redemption, or how functionally insignificant our contribution is.

turn around and trust in the salvation that God lifted up into plain sight through the cross, we can be rescued.

But John 3 isn't mainly about our contribution to Christian conversion. It is really about God's contribution, something theologians call "regeneration." Regeneration is the supernatural remaking of the human heart that happens through a miraculous act of the Holy Spirit. It is the act of God giving new life, freeing us from the stranglehold of our sinful condition, reconnecting us with himself, giving us the spiritual authority to be what we were meant to be and reuniting us with his very being and presence. It is God's work in our conversion, and it is the main work.

The Bible refers to regeneration in many pictures. In 2 Corinthians 5:17, it says that God makes us a "new creation." Ephesians 2:1-7 says we've passed from death to life, a kind of resurrection. It also says that we are refashioned by God as his "workmanship" in Ephesians 2:10. Ezekiel 11:19 and 36:26 say God will take away our "heart of stone" and give us a "heart of flesh." And in 1 Peter 1:3 and here in John 3 regeneration is referred to as the "new birth" or being "born again." *The pictures vary, but the thing that is consistent is the impossibly miraculous nature of what God does. It is a supernatural remaking.* It's like getting a supernatural heart transplant, being raised from the dead, being re-created from scratch or being reborn in the innocent perfection of a newborn baby. That is God's work in salvation. That is the miracle of regeneration.

> Regeneration is the supernatural remaking of the human heart that happens through a miraculous act of the Holy Spirit.

QUESTIONS TO THINK ABOUT

1. Have you experienced real conversion? Have you made a repentant and faithful confession to God in complete and sincere apology? Have you asked him to do the supernatural work of regeneration in you?

2. If you haven't but you are ready to, all you have to do is outlined in Romans 10:9-11:

   That if you confess with your mouth, "Jesus is Lord," and believe in your heart that God raised him from the dead, you will be saved. For it is with your heart that you believe and are justified, and it is with your mouth that you confess and are saved. As the Scripture says, "Anyone who trusts in him will never be put to shame." {Isaiah 28:16}

3. To experience conversion, you simply have to verbally express a heart of repentant faith toward Jesus. It has to be first, **repentant**: fully accepting and admitting we are wrong and sinful and God is right and righteous. Second, it has to put **faith in God**: you put your full trust in Christ's death to save you and in Christ's presence to lead and guide you.

4. If this is all we have to do to be saved, why wouldn't we just go back to the way we were after we are "converted"?

DAY 4

The Effects of Christian Conversion

In the last reading, we looked at how Jesus connects us with God through Christian conversion in John 3. We saw that this event has two contributions: We come to repentance and faith, and God does the supernatural, miraculous work of regeneration. This is what Christians are talking about when they say that they have "been saved," "accepted Christ," "been converted," "been born again," "become a Christ follower," "prayed the sinner's prayer" and so on. It means they've turned away from the demands of their depravity, apologized to God for having lived in that depravity and pledged to trust in Christ's death and resurrection for them, living under his leadership.

I WILL BE WITH YOU

The focus of this week is on our relationship with God; his desire to "be with us" and for us to connect with him. Even God's work of regeneration isn't an end in itself. *Redemption* is the end game: A right, good and just relationship with us and all things. God promises over and over in the Bible to be with us. But the fact that it's constantly repeated suggests we often misunderstand how he is doing it. The idea assumes that his presence can still seem like a lack of presence. The most clear single verse on this is probably Isaiah 43:2:

> *When you pass through the waters, I will be with you; and when you pass through the rivers, they will not sweep over you. When you walk through the fire, you will not be burned; the flames will not set you ablaze.*

Most normal people would ask, "Um, God? Why am I going to be in the middle of a raging river in the first place? Or why would I ever be walking through a fire? Why promise flame retardant and not fire *avoidance*? Why promise wading traction and not low waters or competently constructed bridges?"

God's answer in the Bible seems complex, but he apparently has multiple purposes, including showing who he is to everyone and transforming us in life's painful processes through faith. We'll get to that in the next reading.

Right now, it's important to understand how God is with us actively through the work of Christ, the promises of the Father, and the present work of the Holy Spirit. We have already looked at the *elements* of salvation. Now we need to look at its *effects*.

Christian conversion has two *elements* and four very important *effects*. Understanding these four effects is critical because they are the basis of our ongoing relationship with God. They are the main ways he is with us on a regular basis. They

> Understanding these four effects is critical because they are the basis of our ongoing relationship with God.

are how he relates to us and we relate to him in the new life that comes through his miraculous regenerating work.

We will talk about justification and sanctification the rest of this week and then talk about the indwelling Spirit and spiritual authority in future weeks.

JUSTIFICATION: YOU ARE ACCEPTED IN CHRIST

Justification is technically a legal word. In the Bible it refers to somebody being declared innocent in court, or being pardoned even though they are guilty. Therefore, justification is "the acceptance of believers as righteous in the sight of God through the righteousness of Jesus Christ accounted to them."[1]

God in the person of Christ susbstituted himself and counts the guilt and the penalty of our sin against Christ while giving us Christ's righteousness and standing through

---

1   Richard F. Lovelace, *Dynamics of Spiritual Life: An Evangelical Theology of Renewal* (Downers Grove, IL: IVP Academic, 1979), 90.

THE FOUR EFFECTS
OF CHRISTIAN CONVERSION:[1]

JUSTIFICATION: You are accepted in Christ.

Your relationship is restored. You are counted as just or innocent in his sight. You have been forgiven and reconciled.

SANCTIFICATION: You are free in Christ.

In Christ, you are free from slavery to sin and depravity. You don't have to live in it anymore. It might still feel like you do, but you don't.

THE INDWELLING SPIRIT: You are not alone.

You are spiritually united to Christ himself by the work of his Holy Spirit living in you. He won't abandon you.

SPIRITUAL AUTHORITY: You have authority in Christ.

You have the right to do what he has told us to do. You have the power to stand against spiritual enemies and the power to love human ones.

---

1   Richard F. Lovelace, *Dynamics of Spiritual Life: An Evangelical Theology of Renewal* (Downers Grove, IL: IVP Academic, 1979).

our union with him.[2] Without going into the full dynamics of this, we can just note that justification has the profound *relational* effect of making God's wholehearted acceptance

---

2   People often ask how this exchange of guilt and penalty (what the Bible calls "atonement") works. There are a number of theories, but the most persuasive I have found connects our justification through Christ's atonement to the doctrine of our "union with Christ." We are made one with Christ. We are "in him." Because Christ makes us one with him, we share in his righteousness/position/innocence. His holiness isn't just a screen through which the Father views us. We actually are holy, because we are one with the holy Christ. See Millard Erickson's *Christian Theology*, pg. 836. Another way to understand it is to see guilt as a form of debt (as it is often referred to in the Bible). Debts can be paid and funds credited. We have no logical problem with that. God claims that guilt and righteousness is somewhat like that and so exchange is possible.

of us possible.[3] Christ's death has provided the basis for real forgiveness, or what the Bible calls "expiation," taking sin away. Justification removes the moral obstacle to God's relational acceptance of us.

God's justifying work also includes what the Bible calls "propitiation" (Romans 3:25; 1 John 2:2; 1 John 4:10). That sounds pretty technical, but it isn't. The word "propitious," in a relational context, simply means, "To be favorably disposed toward." So in reference to our relationship with God, it means that God can *like* and *enjoy* us again in a completely morally upright way.[4] The relationship can be completely rehabilitated to the point of fun and enjoyment, of favor and benevolence. This is the result of what is often called "imputation." We have not just been forgiven in Christ, but we have received his moral standing, his righteousness.

The most important clarification about justification is that it is not earned. It is credited. That is, God's acceptance of us is something received and is therefore stable, objective and solid. It doesn't take its stability from our behavioral goodness or justice. It is as stable as the goodness and justice of Christ because *it* is the goodness and justice of Christ.

---

3   If you remember the earlier readings, it is not hard to see how this is profoundly relational. How should a holy God, who perfectly loves all truth and all creation, relate to his image bearers when they are wallowing in their depravity? How does he redeem people who are rebelling in cosmic proportion against all truth at the expense of all creation? Some people don't like God's holiness because they feel restricted by it. It feels like God doesn't want me to be myself. But from a different angle, we see that when I demand that God let me be my depraved self, I'm asking him to change his character, his loves and his holiness, and to stop caring that we be free and whole. I'm also asking him to believe that my right to my depraved condition is more important than my responsibility to embrace my true nature of being made in his image. I'm asking God to change his nature and deny reality. If any of our friends or children were in that dysfunctional of a relationship, we would advise them to get out. Let that person go. We'd tell them, "You'll lose yourself in that relationship. They just want you to enable them." Yet the cross is the very means by which God has proposed to rebuild his relationship with us in a way that allows him to be himself while freeing us to become our real selves. He upholds justice by punishing sin, but he himself bears our punishment. He pays the full cost of forgiveness.

4   You might ask why the Bible doesn't just translate it "God likes us again," but to do so would lose something really important. Propitiation isn't subjective. It isn't based on mood or situation. It's a totally stable favorable disposition. It's more like a property than a feeling. God's propitiousness is much better, more stable and more reliable than our feelings or experience of liking someone.

Sadly, very few people, even very few Christians, really understand what this means. How do you know how the holy God feels about you when he doesn't constantly talk to you like another human being would? Is this God the sort of father who withholds his approval to motivate better performance? No. He is the sort of father who provides for us a perfect ground for his acceptance in order to inspire and enable a beautiful performance motivated by thankfulness and joy and done for all the right reasons.

The reason why many Christians don't feel accepted is because the sinful condition still exists in us in such an obvious way. Even worse, when God regenerates us, our *sensitivity* to our sinful condition *increases* dramatically. The normal human reaction is that instead of enjoying God's promise of acceptance in Christ, we are distracted by our increasing ability to recognize how little we deserve that acceptance. This is actually what is supposed to happen.

We need to understand that this isn't a trade. Good moral performance doesn't equate to God's approval. It is a relationship: God forgives us and accepts us so that we can perform out of the motivation of joy and gratitude. Through knowing God, we learn his loves and pursue them for the right reasons, and in the Spirit, he makes it possible for us to do so. That's what faith and repentance look like day-to-day: learning to distinguish faith from your moral performance and really believing that we are accepted in Christ. Regeneration and conversion happen once. Repenting and believing is sometimes moment by moment.

DAY 5

Sanctification: You Are Free In Christ

READ ROMANS 6:1-23

Offer yourselves to God, as those who have been brought from death to life; and offer the parts of your body to him as instruments of righteousness. For sin shall not be your master, because you are not under law, but under grace.

Romans 6:13-14

Sanctification is a theological word that means to be set apart for God and made like him. It means to become holy. It means to grow not in self-righteousness, but in real righteousness. It is why believers in the Bible aren't commonly called Christians but saints, meaning "holy ones."

That idea does not astound us as it should. Sanctification assumes we are free to become like Christ. It means that the slavery of our sinful condition, our depravity, has been broken by the supernatural work of regeneration and by the presence of God in the Holy Spirit. In Christ, *you are free.* The problem is that you have to believe freedom is possible and actually want to be free.

THE SLAVE'S FREEDOM

We, especially the wealthy West, live in a freedom culture. Commitment and duty are out. Choice and freedom are in. We know deep down that if we make a commitment we might grow bored with what we've chosen and miss an exciting new opportunity that could come along. Freedom, as un-attachment, is king. This is because freedom seems to us more dependable than God in positioning us for consistent happiness.

But according to the Bible, we have it all backwards. In

fact, the first great act of biblical salvation was God delivering people from slavery. *The most fundamental starting point of the Bible is that without God, we're not free: we're slaves.* What was literally true of the Israelites in Egypt[1] is practically true of every life centered in something besides God. This slavery is produced by what the Bible calls "idolatry" and is the breaking of the first commandment: "You will have no other gods before me" (Exodus 20:3). We think of freedom as the ability to do whatever we want to do, but this assumes that we're free to be and want whatever suits us, as long as no one interferes. Freedom is not our natural state; slavery is. And there is nothing more pitiable than a slave who labors under the whips, still in the delusion that he is free because he has somehow come to like something about his bondage.

In truth, we are slaves to sin unless God intervenes.

> But freedom is not our natural state; slavery is.

The strange irony of human life is that we have no ability to be free in and of ourselves. If we demand to be free of God, we will always give ourselves to something, and that something will always be an idol and make us slaves. Only by giving ourselves to God do we find ourselves free to be what we were meant to be with its entire accompanying fulfillment.

The Apostle Paul says it this way in Romans 6:

> [16] *Don't you know that when you offer yourselves to someone to obey him as slaves, you are slaves to the one whom you obey—whether you are slaves to sin, which leads to death, or to obedience, which leads to righteousness? [17]But thanks be to God that, though you used to be slaves to sin, you wholeheartedly obeyed the form of teaching to which you were entrusted... [20] When you were slaves to sin, you were free from the control of righteousness. [21]What benefit did you reap at that time from the things you are now*

---

1   Told in the book of Exodus in the Bible.

ashamed of? Those things result in death! [22]*But now that you have been set free from sin and have become slaves to God, the benefit you reap leads to holiness, and the result is eternal life.* [23] *For the wages of sin is death, but the gift of God is eternal life in Christ Jesus our Lord.*

Verses 20 and 21 could be reworded like this: "When you looked for happiness in something other than Jesus, you were deep into your own thing and free from God's control (just like you wanted to be). Think about those days. Were you really as free as you thought you were? What did you really gain in that lifestyle? Wasn't your freedom really becoming a backward kind of slavery?"

The more the Gospel enlightens your perspective, the more you cringe with shame at the things you thought would make you happy. That old freedom looks like it was really slavery. That's what always happens. That's the secret slavery of sin. This new life is the freedom of God.

To appreciate this, we must understand that *freedom is always a relative thing.* You can never be free from *every*thing or free to do *any*thing. The minute you are something, you aren't something else, and the only way to be radically free is to be nothing at all. This is precisely the blunder of modern thinking.

Many modern folk think that to maximize your freedom you have to keep all of your options open, but this is an absurdity and is the exact reason why this kind of fellow is anxious about all important decisions. This kind of free man could never commit to love because it would require him to lose a million potential lovers (one of which could be better than the one he chose). He can never work because to choose a career would be to lose a thousand others.

If we have only this short life to live, then we had better have only the best experiences and indulge in the perfect uses of our time so that we might be maximally happy. Nothing can be wasted, no potential squandered. This modern freedom is really a subtle kind of atheism.

On the other hand, if we believe that what awaits us at the end of this short life is an eternity of bliss in perfect community and mystical intimacy with the most fascinating and pleasurable being in the universe, then our daily life is not nearly so anxious. We might be a "slave" to this being because we obey him, but such a slave is free to live. We are free to embrace God and all that he has shown us as good, true, beautiful, honorable and admirable in the world. We are maximally free because we are bound only to seek out and labor for good and nothing else. We are only free to be rightly free.

This freedom is also authentic because it is a slavery that is freely chosen on the principle of love, and the Christian man or woman can never be said to be more a slave than God was a slave in making humanity free. Every right action of every Christian is one that she does obediently to her heavenly master, and yet she would freely do for her divine friend and for her own reasons in loving what is good.

It is only by this hidden wisdom of love and friendship that the Bible can speak frankly of redeemed people who are both free and slaves. In one sense we are slaves to God because we obey him. He has that level of authority. Yet we are also people who must never forsake God's great gift of freedom. In Galatians 5:1 Paul says, "It is for freedom that Christ has set us free."

REAL FREEDOM

God only does what is good. Titus 1:2 says we can have confidence that we'll have eternal life because God promised it, and God never lies. He can't. Is God less of a god, or is God a slave to the good because he cannot lie, because he will not lie? Freedom is a good thing because it allows us to do the right thing. Sin enslaves us because it chains us to things that are against our purpose and that pervert the good. It is slavery because it keeps us from acting righteously.

When through Christ we experience regeneration and

the power of the presence of God in the Holy Spirit[2], this bondage to sin is broken. Depravity and sin remain, but they no longer reign.[3] They are still present, but they are no longer in control. You don't have to do those things anymore. In Christ, you are free.

We don't automatically walk totally freely, but we have been emancipated and empowered to live free if we will have a relationship with God. We will find that as we walk with Jesus, we will grow to be like him, and in becoming like him, we will become less unattached and uncommitted because we are becoming something specific. But the loss of freedom that comes from being something definite yields the kind of freedom that is emancipation from the domination and degradation of our being.

The more the Holy Spirit regenerates our conscience, the more unwilling we become to submit to the whip of sin ever again. The further we travel, the more we trust God and put to death the condition of depravity through the Holy Spirit's leadership, the more freedom from sin we will feel, and the more practically free we will be.

FOR FURTHER REFLECTION
2 Corinthians 3:13-18

Ephesians 3:12-21

James 1:23-27

---

2   Romans 6:16-19

3   The idiom, "Sin remains, but doesn't reign" is from John Wesley, a leader of the 18th century English awakening. It is said that this revival accomplished more in England for the better in a bloodless revolution than was accomplished in the secular revolution in France that was called "The Reign of Terror." The Awakening was also what produced the anti-slavery leaders of the next generation, including William Wilberforce and others, who fought toward the abolition of slavery in the West over the following 80 years. It is one of the greatest examples of how a spiritual awakening can radically change the course of peoples and nations for the better.

WEEK 2
CONNECT
WITH OTHERS

The old word for connecting with others in Christ was fellowship. Most contemporary churches, however, refer to the horizontal, relational calling of Christian faith as community. For many, the idea of fellowship conjures up mental pictures of styrofoam coffee cups, fluorescent lights and pale rooms, but for some, it still feels more organic. The word "fellowship" has at least as rich a meaning as the word "community." Fellowship has historically meant a companionship rooted in shared ideas and values, usually in a cause in which people are trying to accomplish something together. Fellowship describes rich friendship engaged in deep action.

Many words seem to lose their gravity over time. Even the deep word "friendship" has come to mean only what "companion" usually meant in the past, and "family" has come into a very wide definition indeed.[1] Fellowship, like family and friendship, is meant to describe a relationship based on a moral and personal commitment that is unwavering and even involuntary. Christian community is a spiritual family, not merely a social network.

But God's assertion that intimate community with himself and other people is the greatest human good has fallen almost into legend. In recent decades, our culture has

---

1   The main problem with the present definition of family is not that it includes arrangements that the Bible teaches are immoral, but that it confuses the involuntary nature of the family. Your family are the people you are related to in everything BUT choice. Family is involuntary. It is chosen for you and cannot be broken by you. What we resent is that we have undeniable responsibilities to people we have not chosen. This is something we have to learn to embrace. It is also one of the things we must learn to embrace about the Church.

moved quickly away from these values, and our acceptance of the idea that faith is *merely* personal has been a most effective destroyer of personal faith. This blunder has gained momentum through the added notion that the Church is not a community but a factory of religious goods and services that one can simply pay for in the offering as though it were a bill.[2] The Church's complicity with these ideas has only accelerated their hold on her and diminished her public reputation so that, in our modern moment, a humiliated Church desperately reaches out to consumeristic people seeking a privatized faith with adjustable doctrines.

> Christian community is a spiritual family, not merely a social network.

This situation is not something that gets better on its own. It is not something we can change without convictional action, and it is not something we can overcome without thinking of the Church and ourselves in a totally different way.

Perhaps the best two pictures God gives us for our nature as a people are the pictures of the body and the bride. In the upcoming readings, we will focus on these two important visions of the Church, then explore what that means for us in today's culture to embrace them fully.

Note: Last week focused on our connection with God and this week focuses on our connection with his people. It may seem like this focus leaves out one of our most central areas of connection—family. However, the connections we will explore will point us back to our most immediate neighbors and most immediate tasks: our families and our work. Our work for provision, the chores of the domestic life and our

---

2 The great irony of this is that giving was meant to increase our allegiance to the community we support together. Once we see the offering as a bill paid to an organization, rather than as a contribution to a family, it is a means of cutting our allegiance to the Church. By paying for the goods and services we use, we free ourselves from obligation.

family relationships constitute the smallest kingdom God has created—the home. When we understand our connection with God and his people, family finds its proper place and purpose.

CONNECT
WITH OTHERS

SERMON NOTES

WEEK 2
CONNECT
WITH OTHERS
SMALL GROUP
DISCUSSION QUESTIONS

WATCH THE SMALL GROUP VIDEO

1. Discuss how you understand the phrase "a culture of anonymity." How do you think this affects community and spiritual health in a church?

2. The Bible is full of "one another," words. Examples[1]:

-to live in harmony with	-to instruct
-to serve	-to encourage
-to be patient with	-to offer hospitality to
-to accept, to be kind to	-to have fellowship with
-to forgive	-to love

   Which of the above "one another" dynamics connect with you the most? Why?

3. What does it look like and feel like to love each other as 1 John 4:11-12 says?

---

1   The Bible also talks a lot about community/fellowship without using the word "fellowship" or "one another."

SMALL GROUP SCRIPTURE STUDY
Ephesians 5:21-33

1 Corinthians 12:1-27

(See Day 1 and Day 2 readings for further comments and insight on these passages.)

1. In what ways do you think these two passages relate to how we connect with others?

2. In what ways should our identity and our individuality interpret who we are as Christians?

3. How do you think the phrase "the whole is greater than the sum of its parts" relates to the Church?

4. What moves you the most in either of these passages? Why?

DAY 1

What We Are To Each Other: The Church as Christ's Body

READ 1 CORINTHIANS 12 *(especially verses 12-27)*

A lot of people say they don't like "organized religion," but I doubt they like disorganized religion either. What I think they really mean is that they don't like public religion. They like their faith good and individualistic. They see faith as more like golf than basketball: it's not a team sport. They think that faith is supposed to be both individual and individualistic.

While I'm not against golf per se, we need to ask ourselves if real, biblical, Jesus-defined faith is that individualistic. Is real spirituality the process of God providing us with goods and services that we desire on our own individual terms? The great church reformer Martin Luther once flatly called individualistic spirituality a sham. He said, "Anyone who is to find Christ must first find the church. How could anyone know where Christ is and what faith is in him unless he knew where his believers are?"[1]

This is all very plain once we clearly understand what Christianity is and is not. Christianity is not a kind of enlightenment. If it were enlightenment, or something that could be pursued individually, then solitary religion or voluntary community might make perfect sense. But God didn't design it this way. Instead, God has tied the working principle of faith to the fiery activity of love toward himself and all people. Love is by definition social, not individual. When we recognize this, we can't help but gather, and the moment we gather in his name, a primitive church is formed. This

---

1 Martin Luther, quoted in "In Defense of Church Hoppers" by Michelle Van Loon, *Christianity Today*, Hermeneutics, www.christianitytoday.com/women2013/january/in-defense-of-church-hoppers.html?paging=off (accessed 15 Jul. 2014).

meaning of "church" built on the working principle of love is Christian spirituality's enlightening idea.

When understood so plainly, "gathered" or even "organized" religion is a badge of honor for the Christian, because the organization is our natural and necessary avenue for living out the love of Christ. We hate the problems in churches the same as everyone else. However, these problems accompany the inclusion of people, and the problem of the Church is also its reason for existing. Seeking a church without problems would be like organizing a hospital where diseases and injuries are just the sort of thing not admitted. The key to a true church is that faith and truth cause the sanity to overcome the sickness. But the devilry of bad religion is always lurking just outside the immediate light of the well-employed saints.

This brings us to the first of two metaphors for the identity of the Church. We are taught in the Bible to think of the Church as a body. This is not a passing idea; it comes up explicitly eight times in the New Testament.[2] This image of us as a body is more than a passing metaphor. The apostle Paul pushes it quite a long way. We are told not only that we are different (as are different body parts), but that these differences are intentional and we are of equal value. We are also told, "Its parts should have equal concern for each other. If one part suffers, every part suffers with it; if one part is honored, every part rejoices with it. Now you are the body of Christ, and each one of you is a part of it" (1 Corinthians 12:25-27). This claim makes the very idea of a consumer organization or a private faith impossible. A body just doesn't allow for that kind of independence. How does one ensure his privacy and independence when he is caring for, suffering with and rejoicing over his fellow body parts? How can he abandon one he is connected to as though by nerves, tendons and flesh? How can we abandon someone we're connected to by the Spirit of Christ?

---

2   1 Corinthians 12:12; Ephesians 1:23, 4:12, 5:30; Colossians 1:18, 1:24, 2:19; Romans 12:4-5.

It's impossible, just as one cannot stub his big toe in the middle of the night and not elicit a reaction from the rest of his body. The very idea is preposterous because humans are intricately connected with a system of nerves that binds our body parts together in shared sensation. It should seem equally unnatural to us to think of a Christian being disconnected from the rest of the body of Christ. Our connection to each other isn't a voluntary addition to our connection with Christ; it is a necessary feature of that identity.

> Our connection to each other isn't a voluntary addition to our connection with Christ; it is a necessary feature of that identity.

For the modern person, this is one of the utterly strange components of authentic Christianity. It is a little like walking into a mall and finding that it is really a monastery, and then, in the strangest circumstances, finding out that the monastery is much more exciting than a mall. It is the realization that wholesomeness is really more satisfying than hullabaloo. It's like a child who realizes that the thing better than his old toy is not another bigger and more exceptional toy to play with on his sterile carpet, but rather an ordinary dog and a great deal of common mud.

Every Christian must eventually embrace this realization, and the sooner the better. It is one of the forgotten keys both to our holiness and to our happiness. We must see the Church as a stroke of divine genius before we can see the worldly wisdom in all its foolishness. And only when our identity is safely in the bridal body can we tell our bodies what they may not attempt to buy: a nice privatized and individualistic religion.

This is the great freedom of being bound to each other. When we become impressed by the very nature of the Church, then we will finally be free from the need for it to impress us.

DAY 2

What We Are To God: The Church as Christ's Bride

READ EPHESIANS 5:21-33

One of the first comments ever recorded about human beings was God's pronouncement that, "It is not good for man to be alone" (Genesis 2:18), and Jesus made no secret about his ultimate purpose: "I will build my church" (Matthew 16:18). As we explored on day one, Jesus' redeeming work was aimed at redeeming not a particular man or woman (though he does that, of course) but a group of men and women who would form a community so intimate that it could best be described as one body (1 Corinthians 12). Until we understand that what we are to Christ we are *together*, the metaphor of being Christ's bride will be largely lost on us.

This body, when described in the Bible in relation to Christ, is called a bride. This relationship points to the final, everlasting union of God with his redeemed people.[1]

Marriage, as a picture of real union, stability, intimacy and community, begins and ends the relational story of the Bible. God drew an intentional connection between his relationship to humanity and the relationship of a husband and a wife. Men and women are to look to the relationship between God and his people for an example of how to live out their covenant of love. If these two covenants of love and union were kept, the world would not be in need of any others.

The picture of the bride is the choice picture of the last book of the Bible, Revelation. The picture is mentioned four

---

1   The bride is "the new Jerusalem" that God has made and that comes down, uniting the new heavens and the new earth (Revelation 21:2). But the inhabitants of the New Jerusalem are the Church, and so this new city is the new house of God with his people. The new city and the new people are one. The difference is that, in the new city, God lives with his people directly.

times in the final chapters. One example is Revelation 19:6-8:

> Then I heard what sounded like a great multitude, like the roar of rushing waters and like loud peals of thunder, shouting: "Hallelujah! For our Lord God Almighty reigns. Let us rejoice and be glad and give him glory! For the wedding of the Lamb has come, and his bride has made herself ready. Fine linen,[2] bright and clean, was given her to wear."

The apostle Paul can't even talk about marriage without explaining how it is bound up in the relationship of Christ and his Church:

> Husbands, love your wives, just as Christ loved the church and gave himself up for her to make her holy, cleansing her by the washing with water through the word, and to present her to himself as a radiant church, without stain or wrinkle or any other blemish, but holy and blameless... After all, no one ever hated his own body, but he feeds and cares for it, just as Christ does the church-- for we are members of his body. "For this reason a man will leave his father and mother and be united to his wife, and the two will become one flesh." This is a profound mystery-- but I am talking about Christ and the church.
>
> Ephesians 5:25-27, 29-32

Human marriage was modeled after the way God intended to be united to his people in Christ from before creation. Therefore, marriage between men and women is meant as an example for us of the union covenant between Christ and his redeemed bride, the Church.

This really should be a stirring thought to us. What is dearer to any man than his bride? Even if a man becomes cynical about his wife, he was never cynical about his bride. However, we should also remember that we are not said to be this bride as individuals, but together as a people.

---

2   "Fine linen" represents the righteous acts of the saints.

With these scriptures in mind, we can see that what we are to God, we are to God *together*. We are not each the brides of Christ, but together we are the bride. We must be his individually, just as the parts of any organism must be alive and connected to the head. But we are not God's completed work on our own, and our individual stories contribute only a single line to the greater story in which we are placed.

None of these observations diminish the individual nature of Christian faith. For the person who says, "Yes, but do we not *ourselves* all have to believe? Is not faith something that must be in every saved *individual*?" Jesus' answer is a resounding, "Yes." The fact that we are the bride of Christ together is not a shot against the individual; it's a shot against the individualist.

> Our individual stories contribute only a single line to the greater story in which we are placed.

The body and the bride are two of the most vivid pictures of our spiritual identity because they are among the most central aspects of our material experience. Though they are different in kind, it should not escape our notice that they are completely compatible, as all brides do have bodies.

Although some men have more trouble connecting to bride imagery, many Christians revel in the idea of being Christ's bride. We rejoice that our union with him will be eternal in its commitment and full of a greater intimacy than that experienced by the most intense lovers or the bravest band of warriors. However, the excitement often cools when we think of sharing that intimacy with every Christian who has ever lived or, more specifically, when we think of sharing it with the very neighbor right beside us. The reality of this union, though, is that this joy will in no way be diminished by our unity with countless other believers. Instead it will be enriched because it is only *with* them that we become Christ's bride. It is only by banding together with the

Church that we grow in Christ into the dear and brightly gowned bride Christ feeds and cares for, and for whom he waits.

FOR FURTHER READING

Stop Dating the Church!: Fall in Love with the Family of God by Joshua Harris.

DAY 3
Community Big and Small

READ ACTS 2:41-47

The theme of this week is that connecting with others is not only *commanded by* God, but it is also a big part of *connecting with* God. One of the ways we love God is by loving others. Honest, deep and dependable relationships are often the means God uses to teach us and bless us. Walking with others is a big part of how he has asked us to walk with him. That's what we mean by community.

HOW COMMUNITY SELF-DESTRUCTS

There is a practical problem, though, with this little equation. If community happens, community tends naturally to self-destruct. When the life of God really comes into people and they start loving and serving each other as they would care for their own body, that gets the attention of other people. And when numerous new people seek to be added to the intimate community, issues inevitably arise. The natural scope of deep relationships can only include a very small number, and this predictable threshold of intimacy can be easily overwhelmed by new people. When this happens, the community faces one of two problems.

If that community ignores the new people, then its love sours and the community becomes ingrown. Its love narrows, and its spiritual vibrancy begins to wilt, because the individuals' love is becoming less missional, and less like Jesus'. We may find ourselves loving people because they mean something to us and forget that we started loving them because they mean something to God.

But if instead, that community embraces those attracted by its intimacy, the arrivals make intimacy impossible by the sheer force of numbers. Intimacy that can be had in a group

65

of 12 cannot be had amidst 120 or 1,200. This is an inevitable problem of growth in healthy spiritual communities.

COMMUNITY BIG AND SMALL

So what can we do when the small community has to grow large? Well, the Bible actually has a good answer for this. While the early churches were mostly small house churches, the very first church was in a similar position to many of our modern churches. Acts 2:41-47 shows this very helpful snapshot of the church in Jerusalem:

> [41]*Those who accepted his message were baptized, and about three thousand were added to their number that day.* [42]*They* **devoted themselves to the apostles' teaching** *and to* **the fellowship**, *to the breaking of bread and* **to prayer**…[44]*All the believers were together and had everything in common.* [45]*Selling their possessions and goods,* **they gave to anyone as he had need**. [46]*Every day they* **continued to meet together** *in the temple courts. They broke* **bread in their homes and ate together with glad and sincere hearts**, [47]*praising God and enjoying the favor of all the people. And the Lord* **added to their number daily** *those who were being saved.*

Verse 46 tells us how they built honest, deep and meaningful relationships, even in a new community with 3,000 new believers that would very soon grow to 5,000. They had two kinds of gatherings. They would meet in the large open spaces in the temple courts to be taught by the apostles, but then they gathered together in homes to eat together, learn, pray and enjoy each other's company.

Verse 41 summarizes what they all committed to at their baptisms. Everyone apparently understood that living out the faith would include at least four things: hearing teaching, fellowship with other believers, the shared meal that included the Lord's Supper and prayer.

This gives us a simple and clear model for a church that grows big and needs to stay small at the same time.

The name we give the two meetings mentioned here are worship and small groups. This is exactly why our church invites everyone to come to Sunday worship and to join a small group.

THE FIVE PURPOSES OF SMALL GROUPS

You can also see in these verses why our small groups have five purposes:[1]

1. **Community/Fellowship:** connecting with others in real spiritual friendship

2. **Study/Discussion:** growing in our understanding of the Gospel and knowledge of the Bible

3. **Prayer:** connecting with God

4. **Mission:** reaching the world

5. **Service:** serving the city

This is not only a Biblical model, but it is also the only thing we have found that works. People often like large churches. They tend to be big for a good reason. They have more specialized people and resources to draw from and have staff for ministries like youth and children.

However, in a large church that is not connected by small groups, community and volunteerism steadily diminishes, and our active love for one another (and therefore for God) suffers. The more people there are, the more each individual sees his own contribution as unnecessary or unnoticeable. Such churches often increase in size while diminishing in

> Living out the faith includes at least four things: hearing teaching, fellowship with other believers, the shared meal that includes the Lord's Supper and prayer.

---

1   See Appendix 1 for more on the Five Purposes of Small Groups.

67

FIVE PURPOSES OF
SMALL GROUPS

COMMUNITY — Meaningful and worthwhile relationships

SPIRITUAL GROWTH — Growing in knowledge of the Gospel and the Bible

PRAYER — Exercising faith and praying church-wide prayers

MISSIONS — Adopt and support a HPC Missionary

SERVE — Participate together in organized service regularly and sacrificially potency.[2] We can't see the needs right in front of us. When the church needs a volunteer, we generally ask a mass of people who assume some other more eager, qualified or salaried person will take up the banner and act.

In contrast, when a small group decides to do something, their members all pool in one room. There is no disconnect in communication and no illusion about who the responsible parties are. Not only do many hands make light work, but sacrifice shared with people we love and enjoy is often hardly a sacrifice. In this way, many people can rise up to attack even a very large task through numerous smaller squads as would an army. Small groups, if led well, are the best way to keep large numbers of people engaged.

I honestly like big churches. I like churches that broadly reach a lot of people. But I also want to be part of a deep and potent church. I want to be part of a church that is moving, one where people both grow deep and reach out far. Don't you?

Very few churches actually have that kind of impact, though. Not only do we not know how to grow big and small at the same time, often we actually don't want to. There are two reasons for this.

TWO DIFFERENT TYPES OF GROWING PAINS

Sometimes we resist the idea of growing "both big and small" because of the time and expectations it adds to our lives. Rather than being part of both a large group and a small group, we'd prefer to have both experiences in the same event. This is especially true for young families with multiple school-age or very young children. But without this commitment, we will rarely grow very deep personally, and the church will lose much of its potential potency as a spiritual force in our city.

---

2   This is the opposite of the goal. The hope is that as a church grows it would have more access to resources in finances and volunteerism to have a powerful effect on the city because it has more than enough resources and manpower for the ministries of the church. Real spiritual life should produce abundance, while gathering a large church often produces scarcity even as it provides efficiency.

Sometimes we don't want our church to grow large because we don't want our intimate and dependable friendships invaded by new people we don't know. It is always painful to allow enjoyable friendships to cool for the sake of the intentional ministry of making new friends. This fear of loss is precisely why most Christian communities grow small and, eventually, dysfunctional and discouraged. The burden of spiritual community is much like the burden of having children. It's definitely a painful and inconvenient disruption to lose your time with and access to your spouse, but you must trust that the sacrifices inherent in welcoming new life are worthwhile when compared with the growth and enrichment it yields and the pleasure it brings to our Father.

Making community a priority always comes with costs and fears. That is why we need a theological, spiritual and moral conviction about community, fellowship and friendship, which is the purpose of readings one, two, four and five of this week. I believe that once that conviction forms, we will experience the reality that being part of a community that is both big and small is the wisest and most effective way to live out connection with God and others.

DAY 4

God's Greatest Gift of Justice and Happiness

READ EPHESIANS 4:4-6

I have been guilty of thinking that the best things in life are *not* free. I've been on some of the best hunting leases and gone offshore fishing on some great boats. I've been on a couple of tremendous vacations and eaten at some perfect restaurants. I've shopped my way to manly pleasure at the sporting goods store. In all these experiences, there is a fairly predictable correlation between leisure paradise and wealth. It's hard not to enjoy leisure and indulgence, and both are usually accessed through wealth. They aren't free.

But our lives do not consist of leisure and luxury. The deepest levels of human joy and heartache come not from recreation, but from our relationships with people as we're engaged in constructive tasks worth doing. *Loving and being loved is the greatest human joy,* and this has been known by all who have either recognized or seen it. In fact, it is usually only the potent distraction of wealth that can confuse this obvious idea. The more permanent, complete and mystical the bonds of this love, the more fulfilling it is.

THE POWER OF A COMMON LOVE AND A PERFECT IDEAL

However, there is a deeper fulfillment that is plainly understood by all men who go together to a sporting shop and by all women together seeking the perfect shoe. The men know that friendship is better when it is focused on a mutually shared interest. Three men are usually more excited when going together to a sporting goods store than those on their way to the grocer because their friendship is enriched by a shared and unifying love. The spiritual application of this social fact is found in Ephesians 4:4-6:

71

There is one body and one Spirit—just as you were called to one hope when you were called—one Lord, one faith, one baptism; one God and Father of all, who is over all and through all and in all.

One of the great dynamics of the Gospel is its ability to join men and women together through a common love. Yet there is another further joy in friendship and romance portrayed by a couple of ladies on an afternoon errand to the shoe shop: the pursuit of a perfect ideal. These women seek the perfect pair of shoes, a thing that does not in fact exist. They wish to purchase something as close as possible to their dream, and that dream is the perfect nexus of the great three female shoe needs: style, comfort and affordability. Every day they are confounded by the reality that every pair of shoes has at most two of these characteristics.

Yet these women are not united by the likelihood of their quest succeeding but by a common belief in the search's goodness. That women should have happy and stylish feet affordably is a goal worth a Saturday afternoon. That Christ redeemed us to redeem the world is an ideal that can rally every believing man and woman until the end of the world.

The overlooked irony of all these plain facts is that they all uniquely converge in Christ's humble but glorious Church. *Within this one community is the convergence of all kinds of people in genuine friendship, sharing an identical love and pursuing a perfect ideal.* It offers not only the potential for friendship by the presence of other people, it unites and directs these friendships through the Gospel itself. The fellowship of friendship is intensified by a shared love of Christ and by the ideals of his name and kingdom being seen and embraced among all people.

When all this is seen through the plain and simple actions of everyday life, it should also be clear that the great pleasures of the Gospel are superior and free. The 300-yard hole-in-one, the perfectly-seasoned filet, the exquisite shoes and The Blue Marlin restaurant in downtown Madison cannot compare in the rightly calibrated heart to the salvation of a single immortal soul. It is the men and women who tire themselves with this proper adventurous and intimate work of service who most joyfully exhale while on the fishing boat or in the salon.

Regardless of anyone's opportunity for great leisure or luxury, the great justice of the Gospel-created Church is that the greatest joys of human life are available in her free of charge and regardless of position. *If the greatest human joy is friendship intensified by a common love in a worthy ideal, then the Gospel is the free and open way for all humanity to take hold of it.*

> Within this one community is the convergence of all kinds of people in genuine friendship, sharing an identical love and pursuing a perfect ideal.

This is why both great happiness and misery are found among the poorest and the richest. It is also the reason why some have observed that the happiness of the poor occurs more often than one would naturally predict, and less among the rich than one would expect. The reason is not that poverty brings happiness, nor that wealth brings misery. The reason is that poverty is focusing by being limiting, and wealth is distracting.

God has structured reality so that the pauper and the heiress have equal access to the better portion of the joyful life. He has very kindly created us so that the obedience we must offer leads to the happiness we cannot neglect. He has made the greatest joys of human life available only within the greatest pursuit of human living: love and service, or in a single word, friendship. The most intimate and fulfilling of all friendships are those bound in common love for Christ's mission and ideal. What shall we call a group of such friendships gathered together to love the Savior and spread together his redemption? I think Jesus would call it a church.

DAY 5

Why You Need A Particular Community

READ HEBREWS 10:25

"We want what we cannot possibly have on the terms that we want it."
                                    - James Davidson Hunter[1]

THAT ANNOYING CONVERSATION

Do you remember dating? I try not to. But have you ever had a conversation with someone in a "flat" relationship? We've all known (or been) someone who was really excited at first, but after a while, the person he or she was dating doesn't seem as interesting and attractive anymore.

The conversation goes something like this: "I really loved her at first. It was like everything was perfect, like we were soul mates. I liked the way she did things. I liked spending time with her. I liked spending money on her. I thought all of her jokes were funny, and I thought everything she said was genuine, but now... I don't know, the whole thing just seems boring, and the things I used to really like mostly just annoy me. And to make it all worse, the other day she asked me for a commitment. I think I kind of blew up at her."

Been there? Well, this sentiment can be felt as easily and often about a church as about a man or a woman.[2] Regarding commitment, our relationship with a church is like all our relationships, and in the technological age of informal relationships, it has never been easier to play the field. I mean, why commit to just one church? Why is commitment

---

1   James Davison Hunter, *The Death of Character: Moral Education in an Age without Good or Evil* (New York: Basic Books, 2000), xv..

2   Josh Harris uses a very similar introduction in his book *Stop Dating the Church: Falling in Love with the Family of God*. I recommend it.

important at all? Every Christian in America can download for free better preaching than what is on tap at their local church. Why marry a church? Why not just date a few of them?

In his book *Stop Dating the Church*, Josh Harris offers three characteristics of a church-dater:

Me-centered: He goes for what he can get. "What can this church offer me?"

Independent: She goes because she's supposed to, but she's careful not to get too involved and entangled, especially with the people.

Critical: He's short on allegiance and quick to find fault. He refers to the church as "you" not "we," and he thinks of its problems as "my inconvenience" and "their problem."

When we allow ourselves to relate to the family of God in this way we cheat ourselves, the Church and the world. This is the reason for the Biblical command in Hebrews 10:25: "Let us not give up meeting together, as some are in the habit of doing, but let us encourage one another—and all the more as you see the Day approaching." But wait, how do we cheat ourselves? It might be clear how low commitment hurts the church, and maybe the world, but how are we cheating ourselves?

GETTING THERE FROM HERE

What we want is to be happy. *But deep and reliable happiness comes from a life of character.*[3] This is one reason why God has demanded holiness (a character that looks, tastes and feels like Jesus[4]). We can't know true happiness without it. When this is true of us, we can be reliably happy in a

---

3 I explain this point more in Week 3, Days 3 and 4. Also see C.S. Lewis' essay "First and Second Things." C. S. Lewis, ed. Walter Hooper, *First and Second Things: Essays on Theology and Ethics* (Collins Fount Paperbacks: London, 1985).

4 This does not produce clones or the loss of individuality. Many differences of personalities, gifts, abilities and interests will remain diverse. We will have varying *individualities* that are expressions of the same *character*. This produces a profound unity and diversity in the body of Christ.

way that adds to the happiness of others rather than being reliant on them. The profound maturity and stability that holiness requires is called character, and it is forged by the Holy Spirit in the fires of discipline.

> The profound maturity and stability that holiness requires is called character, and it is forged by the Holy Spirit in the fires of discipline.

The idea that we need discipline to have character in order to be happy is a tough one to accept. It feels more likely that living a low-commitment, high-indulgence lifestyle will assure happiness,[5] but as James Davidson Hunter says in the quote above, the truth is that we can't get the happiness we want on those terms. To be reliably happy, we need to be holy. The Bible calls coming to that realization "wisdom."[6]

Discipline is by definition a rejection of present freedom to indulge for the later rewards of self-control. The Bible treats self-control as a higher kind of freedom, because most of what enslaves us we either do to our*selves*, or can only overcome by great *self*-exertion. *Self*-exertion and *self*-denial both require abundant *self*-control.

When real faith, self-discipline and moral clarity are combined and empowered by the Holy Spirit, the result is a deep and stable moral character that delivers on holiness

---

5   Both low commitment and high indulgence are popular values designed to overcome restraints that limit embracing "happiness opportunities." The idea is that commitments and morals limit options and can act like fences between us and opportunities for happiness such as new lovers, different options or progress and innovation. They are looked at as restraints that other people have put on us and are therefore resented. But this view is wrong, and it is the reason we need a much deeper and more profound moral education.

6   To test this, do a Bible search on "fool," "foolish," "wise" and "wisdom." You'll see that this idea runs through all of the wisdom scriptures (Job, Psalms, Proverbs, Ecclesiastes, and Song of Songs). The fool is someone who won't understand that happiness and blessedness come from trusting God, mainly in living by his moral commands, especially in self-discipline and moral character. "The fool" is characterized not just by ignorance but *moral defectiveness*. The person of self-discipline and character is wise and lives happily, while the self-indulgent and immoral person lives in both evil and misery. In the long run, foolishness, self-gratification and a lack of discipline destroy people's lives and hurt people around them terribly. That is why morality isn't just right; it's inspiring, loving and beautiful.

and produces happiness for oneself and others.[7]

THE COMPLEXITY OF MORAL CHARACTER

All that is easier said than done. Schools, well designed for teaching things like math, are "astonishingly ineffective" at inculcating moral character in children.[8] The formation of character grows best in the institutions God has designed to work together for this purpose: the family and the Church. This is because the formation of character requires much more than mere instruction on moral rules and their explanations.

In *The Death of Character: Moral Education in an Age without Good and Evil*, James Davison Hunter summarizes the six moral properties (in two categories) necessary for a morally clear conscience and sufficient self-discipline for a godly life.[9]

MORAL CONTENT

1. **Moral Imperatives:** the moral law; knowing what is right and wrong, good and evil

2. **Moral Ideals:** a vision of the moral law lived out that inspires love and devotion; seeing what is good and right as true and beautiful and having a clear mental picture of its flowering in real life

3. **Moral Explanations:** the *reasons* why the moral laws are true and binding, and the *reasons* the moral ideals are worthwhile and inspiring; answering the "why?" questions of morality

---

7   This is hard for most modern people to believe because they don't realize how dependent happiness is on tastes. Our tastes, the basis by which we mentally and emotionally take pleasure in things, tell us what is good, beautiful, interesting, exciting, reprehensible and so on. If our tastes are recalibrated with our conscience in Christ, we will take pleasure in very different things, things that are more accessible, stable, sustainable, mutual, irrevocable (no one can take them from us because they are spiritual) and eternal.

8   Hunter, *Death of Character*, 9.

9   "Character does not require religious faith. But it does require the conviction of truth made sacred, abiding as an authoritative presence within consciousness and life, reinforced by habits institutionalized within a moral community." Hunter, *Death of Character*, 19.

MORAL CHARACTER

4. Moral Discipline: the inner capacity to restrain immoral urges and temptations (self-control or self-discipline)

5. Moral Attachment: loving what is good and seeing it as good, true and beautiful; feeling that to act immorally would be like betraying a lover or best friend (creates strong feeling of duty and shame)

6. Moral Autonomy: the ability to make right choices freely even when under no compulsion or restraint to do so; doing the right thing even when no one is making you do it; overcoming opposition to doing the right thing even when the cost is high

If you're a parent, you might be starting to feel anxious. That seems like a lot. But what is very hard in a classroom happens more holistically and seamlessly in a healthy community of character. These can be taught, modeled, encouraged and disciplined within the natural life of the community of the family and the local church (as long as there is clarity and unity in them). In the classroom, the students greatly outnumber the teachers, but in the community, there are many models, coaches, encouragers and disciplinarians. All are students, all are teachers, and all six lessons converge simultaneously.

THE COMMUNITY OF CHARACTER

This is one critical reason why we need the Church (and the family) and why we cheat ourselves when we date her or consume her goods and services without belonging and commitment. The Church is your God-appointed and Christ-bought spiritual family. *She is a community of faith, but as importantly, she is a family of character.* The Holy Spirit works through close contact with others to make us more like Christ. In close contact with others, he refines us, teaches us deeper faith and encourages us toward true righteousness (not self-righteousness).

LEAVING DATING AND CONSUMING BEHIND

Whenever I have that "Should we break up?" conversation with someone these days, there is one question I always ask: "Is the problem the girl/guy, or is it *the kind of relationship* you're seeking your fulfillment in?" Dating is a funnel, not a bottle. It is an audition, not a play. It is meant to expire so something plainer, yet better, can endure: marriage.

> The Holy Spirit works through close contact with others to make us more like Christ. In close contact with others, he refines us, teaches us deeper faith, and encourages us toward true righteousness.

Similarly, long term happiness cannot be had in an undisciplined and uncommitted relationship. The Bible has always claimed that self-discipline is indispensable to happiness and holiness.[10] Recently, secular psychology has learned that strength of willpower—self-discipline and not self-esteem—is the #1 indicator of future success.[11]

Hebrews 10:25 assumes these disciplines are not attained on one's own but in a community of character: the Church. It calls us to "keep getting together" (be a community) and to "encourage each other" in truth and character. God has made our holiness and happiness contingent on character. He has made what we need (character through community) the way to the reliable happiness we most deeply want.

That is why dating the Church can never replace marrying one. That is one reason you need the Church and it was meant to have you.

---

10   See Proverbs 25:28, 16:32; Galatians 5:23; 1 Corinthians 9:25; 2 Timothy 1:7; Titus 1:8, 2:2; and 2 Peter 1:6

11   Roy F. Baumeister and John Tierney, *Willpower: Rediscovering the Greatest Human Strength* (New York: Penguin Books, 2012), 190-193.

QUESTIONS TO THINK ABOUT

1. **Have you been baptized?** Baptism is publicly confessing that you belong to Christ and his church. *Read more about baptism in Appendix 2.*

2. **Have you considered church membership?** Some people think church membership is unbiblical. The words church membership are never used in the Bible but neither are the words Trinity, infallibility or substitutionary atonement. Yet we believe that Scripture teaches these things. Likewise, we believe that what we call church membership is biblical in light of what the Gospel says about our connection to the family of God. Do you agree or disagree, and why? If you've not become a member of a church, is there a particular reason why?

GROW

The whole of Christian faith and the Church is built on something called the Gospel of Christ. Gospel means good news. Read that again. Most people read over that word "news" without realizing what it means. The Gospel is not a philosophy. It's not a self-help psychology. It's not a moral code or a set of religious rituals. It is the declaration that something happened, and in that sense it is different from every religion the world has ever known.

Dr. Martin Lloyd-Jones was one of the great preachers of the last century. He once explained the "good news" concept this way. Imagine that you live in an ancient country, and your country is being attacked by a foreign king. Your own leaders gather the best warriors and go out to meet the army that is coming to conquer you. After the armies engage, one of two kinds of messengers will be sent back to your city. If the enemy breaks through your army's lines, your leaders will send back advisors. They will advise surrender, a defensive siege or some other course of action, but the success of that action will be up to you. You're going to have to fight for your life.

But if your side wins, different kinds of messengers will be sent. They will bring the "gospel" or "good news." They will tell you news for you to receive, believe and be glad about, and you will be left to respond to that news in whatever way is appropriate. It's not that the news doesn't demand a response; it does. It demands a response of happiness and gratitude. It requires you to think differently about your freedom and what your life is for. The relief and joy would be transforming. You would not be fighting for your life, and you would not be responding to advice. You would be believing news.

Every other religion in the world brings advice. Some bring self-help and spiritual philosophy, promising enlightenment. Others bring rules and moral boundaries to perform, offering divine approval or earthly success. Only the Gospel brings news. It is only Jesus who tells us that we need saving and that he has done the work of it himself. Our salvation is already accomplished; it need only be received. He is the only God who claims to do the supernatural work of transformation through his own power. Only he teaches that the only condition of salvation is rejecting the world of religious self-salvation and trusting the news of his rescue of us through his life, death and resurrection. That rejection is called repentance and that trust is called faith. That is the Gospel. When you believe it, Christian faith will no longer feel like a moralistic religion or a self-help, performance-improvement support group. It will feel like something else altogether, and it will feel that way because it is.

SERMON NOTES

WEEK 3
GROW
UNDERSTAND THE GOSPEL

SMALL GROUP
DISCUSSION QUESTIONS

WATCH THE SMALL GROUP VIDEO

1. In your own words, what is the Gospel?

2. Our culture is given over to a psychological minimization of our sinfulness. How does this affect the way human depravity is understood? How the Gospel is understood?

3. One extreme consequence of misunderstanding the Gospel is behavior modification, or following a list of dos and don'ts (see Luke 11:46; Romans 3:10-11, 22-24). What are your thoughts on this?

4. Another extreme is having no sense of personal depravity, believing that being good enough can get you favor with God and therefore eternal life. What are your thoughts on this?

5. How can understanding the Gospel and human depravity help to address these (and other) consequences?

SMALL GROUP SCRIPTURE STUDY
Romans 3:10-24
Ephesians 2:8

Paul spends the first nine verses in Romans 3 explaining that both Jews and Gentiles are guilty before God. It has nothing to do with how well they follow (or do not follow) directions. Everyone is guilty of something. He then spends the next nine verses proving his claim with three different examples of how people sin, showing that no one can say, "I am not guilty!"

1. In verses 10-12, Paul begins with the sweeping general statement of everyone's guilt. What is he commenting on in terms of one's ability to do good apart from God?

2. In verses 13-14, Paul carries his argument on with specifics to make sure no one is left out. What sin does Paul illustrate of which no one can truthfully say, "I'm not guilty?" Why do you think he chose this? (See Proverbs 10:19; Titus 2:3; James 1:19, 26; and 1 Peter 3:10)

3. The final argument Paul makes for all having some kind of moral guilt before God is in verses 15-18. What is it and what kind of attitude brings this out in people?

4. How would you put each day's reading in your own words?

5. What conclusions can you draw from the readings, and how does it personally resonate with your relationship with God and with the Gospel?

DAY 1
Believing in Grace

READ EPHESIANS 2:1-10

*For it is by grace you have been saved, through faith –
and this not from yourselves, it is the gift of God – not
by works, so that no one can boast.*
Ephesians 2:8-9

The Christian message functions on the principle of grace, a word few people ever use non-religiously. It's too bad. Grace means favor and generosity that comes from the character of the giver and not at all from the merit of the receiver. It is the only way there is ever good news for the undeserving and underperforming. That is, for anyone.

SAVED BY GRACE OR FAITH?

A friend of mine told a story about a class he taught in a Bible school. He asked the class one day, "How are we saved?" They responded dutifully, "We're saved by faith!" It actually says that in Romans 3:28 and other places in the Bible. Yet to the students' horror he said, "No!" And he was right.

We have to know and understand as Christians that we are *not* saved by faith. Only after we understand that rightly can we know that we *are* saved by faith.

Confused? Keep reading.

EMPHASIZING GOD, NOT ME

Whenever we are doing something with someone else, we are prone to remember our part of it. This is especially true if we did not see the other work being done. We are the champions of our own lives, and we are familiar with our own actions and thoughts. So when we come to salvation, we tend to focus on *our* contribution. We think of salvation in terms of what we do and what's required of us, and it is easy to see in the Bible that what is required of us is faith and a life that demonstrates that faith.

But as my friend perceived, over time, this can lead to a very dangerous misunderstanding. *If we see our faith as the means of our salvation, then it is not long before we will be pinning our hopes on and taking pride in our faith.* And this well-meaning way of thinking can lead to the most poisonous form of religion. Believers can take pride in their excellent faith on one day, and the next day be discouraged and anxious that their faith isn't enough. The gospel is supposed to create a joyful and humble people, not a community of people flopping back and forth between neurotic fear and rank pride.

Ephesians 2:1-10 was given to help us be clear about the nature of our salvation, and the emphasis of this passage is completely on *God*. It is important and intentional in these verses that faith is hardly mentioned and our contribution to salvation is treated as nothing. We're supposed to

> The gospel is supposed to create a joyful and humble people, not a community of people flopping back and forth between neurotic fear and rank pride.

see it as nothing. Verses 1-3 pretty well sum up our contribution to the salvation situation:

- We were dead in transgressions/sins.
- We followed the ways of the world and the Devil.
- We followed the dictates of whatever thoughts or desires popped into our heads.
- We were the deserving targets of God's wrath.

It's not exactly pride material, is it? Here, God teaches us that remembering this was our state is much more important than remembering how devoutly we've believed.

> *But because of his great love for us, God, who is rich in mercy, made us alive with Christ even when we*

> *were dead in transgressions—it is by grace you have*
> *been saved.*
>
> Ephesians 2:4-5

Notice the point of the "but" here. The last verse ends with our being objects of destruction – kindling for the fury of God's anger – and rightly so. The Bible is not ashamed to speak of wrath because when it is God's anger, it is perfect. It is completely proper, appropriate, proportional and correct. In John Wesley's collected works, he said of God's wrath that God may well be much better to us than we deserve, but he is never worse to us than our crimes require.

Verse 4 tells the other side of the story, and the verse can be more literally translated: "*But God*, who is very rich in mercy, through his very abundant love, he has loved us..." This story is about how good, merciful and loving God is, but it is also about his power. Verse 5 says that while we were dead in that old life under wrath, he "made us alive" with Christ. And then it says: "It is by grace you have been saved." Grace is simply undeserved, generous favor. It is to say, "You are saved precisely and only because God wanted to save you."

That is the amazing thing. Your faith is not amazing. Your goodness is not amazing. It's not even remarkable. The reason you are saved if you are a Christian, or will be saved if you become one, is because God has made you alive in Christ. The reason he has done this is not your faith, but his favor and his desire. You are redeemed because God wanted to redeem you. *He* is the notable thing. He is the one who makes this story good news for us.

The apostle clarifies in verses 8-9:

> *For it is by grace you have been saved, through*
> *faith—and this not from yourselves, it is the gift of*
> *God—not by works, so that no one can boast.*

There are three clarifications here. First, he contrasts grace and faith, and makes sure we see it is the *grace* and not the *faith* that saves us. Second, he reminds us that even the faith is not from ourselves, and thus is nothing to take pride in. Even the faith through which we are saved is not self-generated. And third, he explicitly says our redemption is "not by works," and then gives us the reason: so that no one can brag about their contribution to their salvation.

This is no small clarification. Although it may appear to be a small theological detail, I assure you that its impact is immense. If we think of ourselves as people saved by faith, we will eventually think of ourselves as self-saved people. We'll eventually think, "Yeah, we were in trouble, but we turned around and made things better. We may have had some bad scrapes in the past, but what God requires is faith, and we have done that, and done it pretty well."

> If we think of ourselves as people saved by faith, we will eventually think of ourselves as self-saved people.

The more we fall into pride about our faith, the more we will take pride in all its trappings. We will think we are doing well because we attend church, give money or read the Bible and pray. And all these good things will erode into an ugly religion that we don't enjoy, that repels the city like the plague and that gravely dishonors our God.

Think about how small-minded it is to want to think highly of ourselves. How good could the story be if we were the heroes? How will we be moved and undone by the greatness of the Gospel if we are somehow at its center? Will we really want to worship God? How will we be forever stunned by those two little words, "But God..." (Ephesians 2:4, ESV[1])? The rich pleasures of humility and self-forgetfulness will elude us.

The very first layer of a Gospel blueprint must create a new fascination with the richness of God's loving mercy and generosity. Only when we stop believing ourselves to

---

1   The New International Version splits these words up in the translation so the sentence reads more easily. But in the original language "But God" starts the verse to emphasize who is doing the loving and saving.

be self-saved through God's suggestion and our good faith can we become an unstoppable force of joyful sacrifice.

The window to the great joy of verses 4 and 5 is believing in verses 1-3. Do you? Have you ever believed that you were rightly an object of God's good anger, that you really were enslaved to your own thoughts and desires, following along with the devils of this world?

In order to be astonished that verse 4 starts with the words, "But God," we must first believe all of these things to be true. If we don't, we will miss out on joy unspeakable, because deep down we think we're pretty good people who made a pretty good decision to believe in Jesus.

FOR FURTHER REFLECTION

Go back to Ephesians 2:1-10 and review its primary focus.

1. Do you think about salvation this way?
2. What are three thoughts that you can regularly remind yourself of to reorder how you see these things in Ephesians 2:1-10?

DAY 2

The Gospel is Not Religion or Moralism

READ LUKE 15:11-32

> *Religion operates on the principle of 'I obey—therefore I am accepted by God.' The basic operating principle of the gospel is, 'I am accepted by God through the work of Jesus Christ—therefore I obey.'*
>
> Tim Keller[1]

> *There is not one in a thousand who does not set his confidence upon the works, expecting by them to win God's favor and anticipate His grace; and so they make a fair [spectacle] of [the works], a thing which God cannot endure, since He has promised His grace freely, and wills that we begin by trusting that grace, and in it perform all works, whatever they may be.*
>
> Martin Luther[2]

Throughout the gospels runs a predictable and recurring story line: Jesus pays attention to someone sinful, and good people get offended. Just as predictable is the reverse story: Jesus rails against the upstanding religious people, and the sinful are encouraged.[3]

A good example of this can be found in Luke 19. Zacchaeus is apparently known as such a bad fellow that not only are the *religious* people offended by Jesus' eating with him, but "all the people" are offended (Luke 19:17). Yet Jesus' graciousness was more than emotional affirmation to

---

1   Tim Keller, *The Prodigal God: Recovering the Heart of the Christian Faith* (New York: Penguin Group, 2008), 114.

2   Martin Luther, *A Treatise on Good Works*, 1520 (Rockville, MD: Serenity Publishers, 2009), 31.

3   Another dynamic is common but often overlooked. Jesus never tells the good, upstanding people to behave more like sinners, and the bad people don't stay the way Jesus found them.

this wicked little man. It had quite an impact. This tax man who had sold his soul for money threw it all away in the moment that Jesus shared his bread.

Everyone in his day knew that Jesus believed in the law and in the morality of the Jewish religion. This was the unspoken boulder they all saw rolling toward them as this man of God strode in their direction. The question in all of their anxious hearts was whether there was any hope for them. Was there any way they could not be crushed? Or, through the eyes of the prodigal son in the story of Luke 15, was there any way home?

Therefore, evident in every word and action of Jesus was the message that mercy wasn't just *needed* by everyone; it was really available to everyone, and it did not come only after a person repented. More often mercy was evident before a sinner repented. This was true of Zacchaeus; this was true of the prodigal son; and this was the story of every demon-possessed person Jesus ever freed. Jesus frees people from the hold of sin and Satan, and then they are able to repent.

Our modern view teaches that graciousness means letting people do what they want and that we need liberation from feelings of guilt and shame rather than from moral sins. We have forgotten Jesus' stern and solid moral backbone. The savior we seek now is one who gives us good thoughts and personal affirmations without evoking any kind of change or repentance. Jesus was not a moralist nor was he a relativist.

Two people can be in the same church doing the same thing with deeply different motivations. Religion and the Gospel flow from two very different hearts. The internal logic of moralistic religion is that God loves us when we obey. This is what the Pharisees taught. But in the Gospel, God shows his love for us first:

> For...*when we were God's enemies, we were reconciled to him through the death of his Son.*
>
> Romans 5:10

When we mistakenly believe that God loves us only after we obey, we cannot help but think he does not love us after we fail. This means that we will always be looking more closely at our behavior than at Christ. If we do well, we will not be able to help feeling prideful against worse achievers. And when we fail, we cannot help but be overcome by despair. If suffering comes, we'll either be mad that God let this happen even though we were doing our job, or we'll assume we're being punished for not living up to his standards. When we get criticized, because our sense of security is in our achievements and goodness, the criticism will be devastating. The better we think we are at something, the more devastating the criticism will be, and the more enraged we will feel at someone who dares criticize us.

One pernicious result of this pride is that we will assume that God loves people like us more than people not like us. Since we will naturally put our hope in what we are good at, we will assume other people like us are on the right track as well, and so religion can lead to all kinds of prejudice and bigotry.

The Gospel, however, does not function under these principles. In the Gospel, we realize that our acceptance is completely dependent upon what Jesus Christ has done for us. Our identity rests securely in our union with Christ. God loves and accepts us as radically as he does Jesus because Jesus has joined us to himself. Everything that was his is ours. We can endure suffering for the love of the one who suffered for us, trusting that he will use it for our good and for his glory. Criticism and personal failure may still wound us, but we can accept it because it does not threaten the heart of our peace and personal worth.

When we know that Jesus is the hero of the Gospel story rather than us, we begin to understand that there is no group or kind of person outside of God's love and redeeming purposes. This realization helps us fight our inner prejudices and bigotries.

One other influence of our culture lies in our gravitation toward self-help or therapeutic theology. This theology

RELIGION	GOSPEL
I obey; therefore, I'm accepted	I'm accepted; therefore, I obey
Motivated by fear of rejection or pride in achievement	Motivated by thankfulness and joy
Suffering is unacceptable and evokes anger or depression	Suffering is acceptable and it is painful but not discouraging
Criticism evokes rage and personal devastation	Criticism evokes humility and growth
I have rights with God because I have done my duty	God gave everything for me and could ask anything of me
I am superior to non-achievers	Jesus is the only achiever
God really only loves religious people	God loves all kinds of people

reassures us that Jesus came primarily to make us feel good. We'll talk more about this in tomorrow's reading. For today, consider to what extent you are still functioning on the principles of religion instead of the Gospel. And remember that you can have all of your doctrines right about the Gospel while your heart's motivations are still in the stranglehold of religion. An easy test is that if we commonly feel pride, fear, anxiety or despair as the emotions our faith brings out, then the principles of religion are somewhere lodged in our heart.

FOR FURTHER REFLECTION
Reread Luke 15:25-32. This time pay attention not to the younger brother, but to the arrogance and religion of the older brother.

1. What was Jesus trying to say through this character?
2. How does Jesus expose his hypocrisy and spiritual weakness?
3. What in the story points to God's love for moralistic and legalistic-hearted people?

DAY 3

The Gospel is Not Therapy

READ LUKE 17:11-19

In Day 1, we introduced the two most common misunderstandings of the Gospel. The first was what I called "religion" in the negative sense of being legalistic and moralistic. Today, we'll look at the opposite error, the assumption that Jesus is just here to make us feel better. It is the idea that his job is mainly to give us a good, pain-free and prosperous life and to make us feel good about ourselves and our problems. If he's good and he's nice, then it follows that he can and should be nice to us, right?

This mentality is not an uncommon storyline in the Bible. One story recorded in the Gospels exposes an attitude that particularly parallels our modern expectations. Luke 17:11-19 tells of ten lepers who come to Jesus for healing. He sends them away, and they find that as they go, they are healed. One of them, the non-Jew, returns to Jesus and thanks him, but the others never show. They came to Jesus for healing. It didn't occur to them even to thank him, much less to come to him for salvation.

These people who were healed and missed Jesus are the same tragic figures as people who come to church only to receive encouragement and happy feelings. Jesus came to show us that the Gospel, his good news, was neither the legalistic religion of the Pharisees, nor the consumable healing of the nine lepers. It is something else all together.

These two errors are our defaults, and we need to be vigilantly on guard against them. Moralistic religion (believing we can earn our own redemption) is the natural pattern of the human heart through the ages, and self-help therapy spirituality is the assumption of our particular age and culture.[1] These false religions are always at the doors of our hearts, waiting for a chance to creep back in.

We read a similar story in John 5. Jesus heals a man at the pool of Bethesda, and the man apparently leaves and goes right back to a lifestyle that may have contributed to his sickness. He consumed Jesus' goods and services, but he was not transformed by a relationship with Christ on Jesus' own terms. This storyline is perhaps the most tragic in the Gospels. He was so close, he experienced God's power in his body, and then was so self-absorbed that he missed the greater gift of Jesus himself.

> Jesus came to show us that the Gospel, his good news, was neither the legalistic religion of the Pharisees, nor the consumable healing of the nine lepers. It is something else all together.

This is not merely the storyline of a few Gospel passages, but it is the major theme of the whole Old Testament and the predictable behavior of all of humanity. Using God without living in relationship with him is the reason why God's people were constantly complaining in the desert. It's the sin of Achan in Joshua. It's the cycle of the book of Judges. It's the fall of Saul, Israel's first king, and the undoing of the usurper Absalom. The pattern holds true again, and again, and again, through the whole of our history with God.

While it's easy enough to identify this tragedy in Scripture, we are often oblivious to it in ourselves. One of the reasons this is the case is because the therapeutic mentality is assumed or presumed in our culture. People don't argue

---

1 I am not saying here that religion and therapy have only negative meanings. Religion can also simply mean a set of beliefs about God, and when used this way, there is nothing bad about it. Here I am using it to mean a religious expression that is legalistic and moralistic. When I say therapeutic here I am using it in the self-help, self-focused, popular me-focused sense. I am not talking about therapy based on cognitive science that helps people overcome real mental brokenness for the glory of God. Our topic here is the popular mentality, not the mental professions rightly practiced.

that God should exist for our needs and submit to our desires. They simply assume it. The idea that this could be a badly mistaken notion is considered old fashioned and even morally dangerous.

This wave has been steadily building for more than 130 years and has broken over us with full force in the last 40 years. Unless we understand how abnormal the modern mind is, we will never be really open to the idea that there is something very wrong with our mentality.

If you were to come across a happiness manual written prior to about 1880, you would likely have found yourself reading a manual on morals and manners. This is because, for civilized history, it was commonly understood that the way to be happy was to be good. Being good, as a category, had much to do with one's role in the community, and manners had everything to do with how we treated others. Standards of behavior were built on an assumption that, if the town and community stuck together, life would be better. So, as late as the mid-1900s most people had the mentality that they were here to serve and even sacrifice for others.

By the middle of the 1970s there had been a "tidal shift" in the way most Americans thought about the purpose of life, and the statistical majority began seeking self-fulfillment as their ultimate goal in life. By the late 1970s, 72% of Americans reported spending "much time thinking about themselves and their inner lives."[2] Following the disestablishment 60s, the late 70s and early 80s became known as the "me-decade." And why not? If you have disconnected yourself from the "establishment" (i.e. the community), then you think of yourself as outside the community, free to be whoever you want to be.

The rejection of hierarchies included the rejection of duty and the sense of guilt that went along with it. The rebellion against guilt and shame, which began even before Freud, became the new mode of thinking about our inner

---

2 Donald Whitney, *Spiritual Disciplines Within the Church: Participating Fully in the Body of Christ* (Chicago: Moody, 1996), 9.

lives. If something made us feel bad or guilty, then we weren't thinking about it rightly. We needed to be more free, whether by the rejection of moral norms or by the extreme use of drugs.

Whatever else the liabilities of this shift, it has made the common man in the street think that the idea of a sovereign God, who is king over all and to whom we owe love and obedience, is ridiculous. The self-centered therapeutic mentality acknowledges no limitations to its freedom to seek self-fulfillment and personal pleasure. It rejects any law that could lead to guilt or fear, and it will not submit to the idea that our lives are dependent on any god or even any community.

So why does all this matter for us? It matters because realizing how extreme and unnatural the modern mind has become is one of the first steps to real healing. And any insight into how unhinged we are in this era must come not from the present mob but from the past.

> The Gospel is not the notion that God is like a grandparent taking little Johnny to Disneyland, hovering about to see what passing fancy of ours he can satisfy next.

The Gospel is not the good news that God is going to give you everything you want. The Gospel is not the good news that you are perfect just the way you are. The Gospel is neither the belief that you have nothing to be ashamed of or feel guilty about nor is it the notion that God really does owe you a nice and happy life free of cancer, divorce, abuse and unemployment. The Gospel is not the notion that God is like a grandparent taking little Johnny to Disneyland, hovering about to see what passing fancy of ours he can satisfy next.

Until we understand how far the Gospel is from this present mentality, the Gospel won't make sense to us. We cannot listen to it profitably. We cannot understand its true remedies. All of its loving aid sounds controlling and impossibly outdated.

The therapeutic mind seeks affirmation from God.

God offers forgiveness.

The therapeutic mind seeks internal peace.

God invites us to focus on others, and the result is that he gets us out of our own neurotic heads.

The therapeutic mind wants things to be easy.

God wants things to be good. Because they are not, our work is not always easy.

The therapeutic mind wants to be happy now.

God wants us to be eternally and perfectly happy, and he knows this can only be the result of true and deep holiness in union with Christ.

If this is true, we can recognize God's grace to us even in the worst of times. The prodigal son found grace even in eating the pig's food, for it was there that he awoke from his coma of selfishness and realized that his supposed freedom was actually slavery and a rejection of the one to whom he properly belonged.

It is not until we have this experience that we can really be on our way back home. Only through the daily rejection of the therapeutic mind can we begin to know the mind of Christ and the liberty of belonging to the One who does give true freedom from guilt and shame, and who brings great, deep and pure happiness.

DAY 4

The Deeper Issue:
A Different Way to Think About Sins

> When I have learnt to love God better than my earthly
> dearest, I shall love my earthly dearest better than I
> do now. In so far as I learn to love my earthly dearest
> at the expense of God and instead of God, I shall be
> moving towards the state in which I shall not love my
> earthly dearest at all. When first things are put first,
> second things are not suppressed but increased.
>
> C.S. Lewis[1]

READ MATTHEW 6:25-34

For many pious people, this is a favorite verse: "But seek first his kingdom and his righteousness, and all these things will be given to you as well" (Matthew 6:33). However for the not-so-pious (like the rest of us), this sounds like a dangerous verse. It sounds like we are to seek God's kingdom and trust God to seek our needs and enjoyments, but we might fear that God may not be as motivated about our enjoyments as we think he should be. We have all seen very religious people, and many of them do not seem to be enjoying themselves at all. You may be tempted to think that this seems like one of those spiritual ideas that is impractical in what we call "real life."

Just for a few minutes, consider the possibility that this mystical instruction of Jesus has a completely practical reason behind it. That reason is that the way to fully experience most everything we want to experience is not by seeking the things directly, but by seeking something else.

We want intimacy. But no one who seeks intimacy for its own sake finds it for long. We want to be happy, but

---

1   C.S. Lewis, *The Collected Letters of C.S. Lewis*, III (New York: Harper Collins, 2007), 247.

those who are constantly trying to be happy are among the world's most miserable people. Very few people who do things to be significant find themselves feeling significant. It is very common for those seeking peace from stress to be riddled with anxiety, and for the most devout thrill seekers to be bored out of their minds. Nearly every true pleasure we chase after comes as the product or accompaniment of something else and vanishes like mist when we seek the thing itself.

C.S. Lewis called this the paradox of "first and second things" in an essay by that title. If you want the pleasure of sublime beauty, seek the sunset, the sea or the mountain vista. If you want the greatest pleasure from food, work up a good appetite. If you want great sex or great sport, do it for the love of your spouse and for competition. In the end, you will find that the more you forget about your pleasures, the more they will find you. And if you want everything, seek the only One who is common to all, the Savior and Creator, and his great kingdom of righteousness.

You see, what seems like mysticism in the mouth of Jesus is simply a practical principle that runs all through real life. Seek the right thing, and you find everything. Seek the wrong thing, and you find nothing. The misunderstanding of this point is the dirty little secret of modern, affluent unhappiness. But the proper understanding of it is the gigantic happiness secret of the Gospel.

The inversion of these things, dependent things (second things) with ultimate things (first things), is called something different in the Bible. In the Bible, proper devotion to first things (God) is called "worship." Devotion to something that isn't ultimate is called "idolatry."

FOR FURTHER READING

C.S. Lewis, "First and Second Things"[2]

---

2   C. S. Lewis, ed. Walter Hooper, *First and Second Things: Essays on Theology and Ethics* (Collins Fount Paperbacks: London, 1985).

DAY 5
Eternity: How Heaven Changes Earth Now

*We always thank God, the Father of our Lord Jesus Christ, when we pray for you, because **we have heard of your** faith in Christ Jesus and of the **love you have for all the saints**-- the faith and **love that spring from the hope that is stored up for you in heaven** and that you have already heard about in the word of truth, the gospel that has come to you.*

-Apostle Paul / Holy Spirit, Colossians 1:3-6

The problem with the church today is not that there are too many people who are passionately in love with heaven. Name three! The problem is not that professing Christians are retreating from the world, spending half their days reading Scripture and the other half singing about their pleasures in God all the while indifferent to the needs of the world. The problem is that professing Christians are spending ten minutes reading Scripture and then half their day making money and the other half enjoying and repairing what they spend it on. It is not heavenly-mindedness that hinders love. It is worldly-mindedness that hinders love, even when it is disguised by a religious routine on the weekend. -John Piper[1]

DOES A HOPE IN HEAVEN PRODUCE LOVE OR ESCAPISM?

I remember hearing the statement in my youth that so-and-so is, "so heavenly minded that they are no earthly good." In college I read what Karl Marx had written

---

1   John Piper, "The Fruit of Hope: Love," *Desiring God*, Desiring God Foundation, http://www.desiringgod.org/sermons/the-fruit-of-hope-love (accessed 15 Jul. 2014).

(repeated by Lenin[2] and innumerable others since 1844), "Religion is…opium for the people." This common cliché means that the religious person has no care for the things of the world, even the most practical things. Marx meant there could be no social revolution for equality and justice as long as people thought they would find a better life after this "real" one.

Both the cliché and the claim are, in reality, wildly false. The alternative to religion, irreligion, is no better and probably much worse for achieving justice, equality and harmony in the "real" world. The irreligious have shown no moral superiority in any of the things Lenin or Marx hoped would be cured if religion declined.

Conversely, most of the great social reformers have been religious and have made great sacrifices in this life *because* of their faith, including their faith in heaven. In repeated studies, religious people in general and Bible-believing Christians in particular are the most generous in volunteering time and giving money for the good of others.[3] One typical study found that religious people were 25% more likely to give and 23% more likely to volunteer. Furthermore, when asked *how much* they gave, the average religious person gave 345% more than their irreligious counterpart ($2,210 vs. $642) even though their irreligious counterparts often made much more money.[4] These sorts of Christians all believe in heaven.

Yet the claim lingers, partly because there is some truth

---

2 "Those who toil and live in want all their lives are taught by religion to be submissive and patient while here on earth, and to take comfort in the hope of a heavenly reward. But those who live by the labor of others are taught by religion to practice charity while on earth, thus offering them a very cheap way of justifying their entire existence as exploiters and selling them, at a moderate price, tickets to well-being in heaven. Religion is opium for the people." Vladimir Lenin, *Collected Works* (1905), excerpted, Marxists Internet Archive, https://www.marxists.org/archive/lenin/works/1905/dec/03.htm (accessed 15 Jul. 2014), par. 2.

3 For further reading on this, see various works by Bradley Wright.

4 Arthur C. Brooks, *Who Really Cares: The Surprising Truth about Compassionate Conservatism* (New York: Basic Books, 2006), 34. Brooks argues that irreligious people are more generous with pooled money through government, but much less generous directly out of their personal funds.

in it. A thin layer of religion over a worldly-minded, self-centered heart will produce a kind of escapism that avoids risk and tolerates injustice. Religion is a structure that can be used to keep an evil social order in place or other people's problems out of your life. In 1848 Canon Charles Kingsley said of the truth in Marx's quote, "We have used the Bible as if it were nothing but a special police manual, a sedative (opium) dose for keeping people we treat like livestock patient while they were being overloaded, a mere book to keep the poor in order."[5]

> It turns out selfishness is a human problem rather than just a religious one.

It is painfully clear from history that sometimes the selfishness of people who identify as Christians obscures the transformational power of the Gospel by burying it under moralism and self-affirmation. Faith, the Bible and the Church have been wielded for purposes that are the opposite of their real aim. Yet this is as much a testimony to the depth of human selfishness as to the weakness of faith insufficiently focused on the Gospel of Christ.

THE ROOT OF THE PROBLEM

Saying that religious faith has sometimes failed to produce change and even been appropriated by human selfishness only tells us that many who use the faith for their ends don't believe it or have yet to hear it. If religion were the problem, we would expect not only to see religious people being more selfish because of faith, but also to see an absence of selfishness among the irreligious. Neither of these has a shred of evidence in its favor.[6]

---

5   Language updated. Actual quote: "We have used the Bible as if it were a mere special constable's hand book, an opium dose for keeping beasts of burden patient while they were being overloaded, a mere book to keep the poor in order." Charles Kingsley, quoted in Charles W. Stubbs, *Charles Kingsley and the Christian Social Movement* (Chicago: Stone, 1899), 118-120.

6   Saying there is no evidence in favor of this doesn't mean that no examples of it can be found. Some people will hear about heaven and selfishly use the idea to confirm their desire to be escapist or apathetic. But this is not a rational interpretation of the biblical teaching and not the normal effect of the doctrine received as part of the whole message of Jesus.

It turns out selfishness is a human problem rather than just a religious one. Self-preservation, self-promotion and self-centeredness are found in every human self, starting at about age two. The question is whether this focus on self needs to be conquered, and if so, *how?*

Faith, and faith in heaven specifically, is one of the greatest motivators of self-sacrifice. Faith in heaven frees us from the choke-hold of self-preservation because when we know we are the object of God's all-powerful and loving eternal preservation, we no longer have to self-advocate for it. We don't need to fight to ensure our well-being, secure our futures, prove our significance or garner affection, and we recognize that we could never have won that fight to begin with. Our present and our future are secure in Christ. Since we are assured of his perfect attention to ourselves, we are freed from the futility of a self-focused life. When we are freed from the project of preserving *our interests,* we learn the true liberty of self-sacrifice in pursuit of *his desires.* We are never more free than when we cast ourselves aside in service to his work of repairing and restoring his world.

> Faith, and faith in heaven specifically, is one of the greatest motivators of self-sacrifice.

When the risen Christ assures us of the promise of heaven, he subdues the voice of self-preservation and makes sensible the greatest need for real change: the willingness to risk. Because heaven offers a real life, we can risk our lives even to a real death. Since heaven will include real eternal happiness and bliss, we can endure purposefully both pain and trial for a time that is momentary by comparison (2 Corinthians 4:17). Jesus puts into perspective both our sinful idolatry over our lives and our narrow vision of time.

DON'T LOVE THE WORLD SO MUCH THAT YOU CAN'T LOVE THE WORLD

This means that a gospel-centered view of heaven allows us to accept Jesus' view of this world. That is, we can love the world while not being worldly. Jesus loved those in the world enough to sacrifice for their good and yet didn't love the world in a way that made him unwilling to sacrifice himself for it. The truly redemptive person must love the world in one way and despise it in another. She must love it for what it is, is meant to be and is meant for. She must seek to bring out and redeem the world's purpose and potential. But we must also despise its condition, hating its degradation and the way it is misused and worshiped.

Hope makes risk desirable and trouble endurable. The Christian hope of heaven is not merely that one day all things will go right for us, but that one day all things will be made right. In this world, we live for the purposes of that world. Our hearts must be captured by the one who makes all things right in a world gone wrong, even if we fight in what looks like the long defeat. Pastor John Piper says it this way:

> *Only one thing satisfies the heart whose treasure is in heaven: doing the works of heaven. And heaven is a world of love! It is not the cords of heaven that bind the hands of love. It is the love of money and leisure and comfort and praise—these are the cords that bind the hands of love. And the power to sever these cords is Christian hope.[7]*

Hope in the risen Christ who promised heaven produces joy. But does it produce love? Yes. Heaven is Jesus' vision of his own love's accomplishment and application.[8] It is what his love has bought and will produce. When we see what heaven is to Christ and what it really means for us, an unblushing hope in the reality of heaven can make us the

---

7   Piper, "The Fruit of Hope: Love."

8   Ephesians 2:6 says we were "raised up with Christ…in the heavenly realms," meaning our destiny to be in heaven is assured; we are already its citizens. But we are not often shocked by the next line. Why did he do this? Just to save us from wrath (Ephesians 2:3)? It says he did it "in order that in the coming ages he might show the incomparable riches of his grace, expressed in his kindness to us in Christ Jesus" (2:7). God will be doing in us forever what he has done in Christ: expressing and demonstrating his incomparable riches and generosity as demonstrated in Christ.

most earthly good that a person can possibly be. We will be interested not only in the eternal happiness of all people, but we will be driven to live for the good of all people. We will want to see God's will done "on earth as it is in heaven" (Matthew 6:10). True faith creates passionate imitation of the beauty of Christ, especially his moral beauty. Heaven is what his self-sacrificial love will produce, and therefore self-sacrificial love will be the spontaneous reaction and disciplined passion of all of heaven's true citizens in imitation of their true king.

FOR FURTHER REFLECTION

John Piper's sermon, "The Fruit of Hope: Love" is available on his website: *www.desiringgod.org.*

Find a link at *hpcmadison.com/blueprint.*

GROW
KNOW THE BIBLE

There are three feelings or attitudes I hear expressed over and over about the Bible. The first is **modern cynicism**. People assume that a book as old (read: "primitive") as the Bible can't tell us how to live in the present or launch us into a better future. The second is the feeling of **intimidation**. People say they have trouble understanding the Bible. They say they don't know where to start. They say that the kind of writing and the ancient idioms make it difficult to read. But the third is just as common: knowing the Bible **has great value**. I've talked to hundreds of people who have openly told me that reading the Bible—knowing it and studying it—was perhaps the best decision they ever made.

I know from personally shepherding people within numerous ministry contexts that it is when people learn to read and understand the Bible for themselves that they begin to grow dramatically in their faith in Christ. Although most people first come to faith through a relationship with a Christian friend, it is when they begin to read the Bible for themselves that they really begin to know the Christ they have decided to follow and who they are in him.

Once people choose not to be intimidated by the Bible, but to find the help they need to read and understand it, they find it to be much more understandable than they expected. They find that with a little background knowledge, most passages are quite easy to understand. They also realize that the places that require extra effort to mine often yield jewels of wisdom and knowledge of God that are well worth the effort.

When this happens, cynicism usually decreases. Most

find a timelessness in the ancient text similar to the time-lessness of the God who stands behind it. They find that the Bible is what it claims to be and does what it claims to do. It is the written word of God, and it makes the simple[1] wise.

Knowing the Bible is a key to Christian growth, and it's one that you'll likely find both pleasurable and meaningful.

---

1   In this context "simple" means naïve, foolish, inexperienced, moderately un-intelligent, unschooled or unsophisticated. It refers to anyone who needs insight and wisdom (see Psalm 19:7).

GROW
KNOW THE BIBLE

SERMON NOTES

GROW
KNOW THE BIBLE
SMALL GROUP
DISCUSSION QUESTIONS

WATCH THE SMALL GROUP VIDEO

1. What about the Bible most intimidates or intimidated you?
2. Which is harder for you:
    a. Reading the Bible or wanting to read it
    b. Finding and making time to read it
3. Knowing the Bible is not a function of intelligence or education.
    a. Do you think that's right?
    b. Was Martin Luther right that the common peasant could understand the Bible? Why?

SMALL GROUP SCRIPTURE STUDY
2 Timothy 3:16

1. Knowing that every book in the Bible has a human author and a divine author, what does it mean that all Scripture is "inspired by God" or "God-breathed"?[1]
2. How does knowing this affect your approach to the Bible?

---

1   "God-breathed" is the more literal translation.

3. In what ways has the church helped you get to know the Bible?

    a. What have your experiences been (good and bad)?

    b. Which have been the most helpful and why?

4. Application: Nic said do something:

    a. Realistic

    b. Practical

    c. Habitual

What might this look like for you?

SMALL GROUP SCRIPTURE STUDY

Isaiah 55 *(especially verses 10-11)*

For more on Isaiah 55, see HPC sermon from February 2, 2014

1. What is God's message in this passage?

    a. What does he explicitly say about his word?

    b. What does he say through the picture of rain and crops?

2. This passage is specifically referring to God's prophetic word in the oracles. But what here applies to all of his words, including his written word? Is there anything that does not apply?

3. How do verses 8-9 relate to verses 10-11?

If you get stumped, see the discussion of Isaiah 55 in the reading for day two of this week.

SMALL GROUP SCRIPTURE STUDY

2 Timothy 3:16-4:2

There are two lists in these verses of the uses of Scripture:

    a. Teach, rebuke, correct, train

    b. Correct, rebuke, encourage

1. Why do you think Paul uses such "serious business" words?

2. Can you give an example of a time when you were _____ by Scripture?

   a. taught or trained

   b. rebuked or corrected

   c. encouraged

2. What do your answers tell you? Was it easy to think of times the Bible confronted and changed you, or was it easier to think of times it encouraged or comforted you?

DAY 1

What The Bible Is:
A Pointer to Christ

In the beginning was the Word, and the Word was with God, and the Word was God. He was with God in the beginning.
John 1:1-2

The man who saw it has given testimony, and his testimony is true. He knows that he tells the truth, and he testifies so that you also may believe.
John 19:35

THE SORT OF THING A THING IS, IS IMPORTANT

The Bible claims that it is the written word of God, his inspired communication, and is itself, "God-breathed" (2 Timothy 3:16). If we believe this, is it possible to think too highly of the Bible? Is that a trick question? Yes, it is.

For example, I could think very highly of a chef named Jane. And I could say of her, "Why, she is the greatest chef I know of, and I suspect the greatest chef in the entire world. She may even be the best that has ever lived."

This sort of praise is probably foolish, but it is at least the right *sort* of praise. That is because no matter how absolutely I admire this chef named Jane, I am admiring her as a chef and not as an emperor. It would not be the appropriate kind of praise if, after eating an exquisite meal, I stood up and said, "This duck was so perfect an entrée that we should all storm City Hall and make Jane mayor!" or "This filet is grilled and seasoned to such perfection that henceforth Jane shall be my priest." The obvious fact here is that even the greatest things can only be what they are. To forget this fact is to destroy things precisely when we think we are promoting them.

This tendency to promote things to their destruction is a common temptation to anyone who comes to see how great and divine the Bible is. To have in our hands a written repository of God's revelation to humanity is perhaps among the most stunning bits of news human beings have received. This news can create two opposite blunders. The first is to simply assume the claim is too good to be true and not believe it. The second is to make it a god. That is, not just to promote it as God's written word but to praise the scriptures as a higher entity in and of itself.

Sound weird? This is the exact error of some of the religious people of Jesus' time. The first verses of John tell us plainly that the fullest and greatest expression of the Word of God is in the Son, Jesus, who became the Savior. The Bible, as John says of his own writing in John 19:35, is the true testimony *pointing to* the One who saves us. It is written and given to us, "so that you might believe."

This is exactly what these very intelligent and devout people missed. They loved the Bible but were unable to believe in the one to whom it pointed: Jesus. So Jesus told them in John 5:39-40:

> *You diligently study the Scriptures[1] because you think that by them you possess eternal life. These are the Scriptures that testify about me, yet you refuse to come to me to have life.*

The Bible had become an end in itself. It had become a kind of god, and they had made the word into a system of beliefs and practices to gain salvation, leaving no room for belief in the actual Savior.

THE PURPOSE OF POINTING

One of the most annoying things about training a dog is that pointing usually doesn't do any good at first. You can point at something, but most dogs will just stare, bewildered at your finger. Pointing can distract the animal from

---

1   "Scriptures" literally means "writings." Jesus is referring to the writings that make up the Old Testament of the Bible, since the New Testament hadn't been written yet. But what is true about God's intent in any part of Scripture (divinely inspired revelation) is true of all Scripture, both the Old and New Testaments.

what you are pointing out. The pointing becomes an end in itself and doesn't direct the animal to what you want it to see. They don't understand that the pointing is intended to direct their attention to something else.

The Bible points to Christ, and it is in him that we have life. Whenever we read it, we are not seeking the Bible, or even wisdom or theology. We are seeking God, and everything we learn is to point us to that end. We read the Bible because we are seeking to know God and to honor him by applying the Gospel.

THE PART THAT POINTS TO US

There is another type of "pointing" in the Bible that we too often miss. We sometimes read the Bible and then get frustrated with the Jewish people in biblical times. They seem to be constantly making and re-making the most foolish mistakes. It is tempting to see them as a morally defective group of people, incapable of obeying the most basic commands. They *are*

> It is easy to judge the biblical examples, but when we do, we miss the reality that they are pointing to us.

profoundly defective but not for the reason prejudice would tell us.

The point of the Bible's record of the Jewish people is not to show us the *defective behavior of a particular ethnicity*, but the *defective behavior of typical humanity*. It is easy to judge the biblical examples, but when we do, we miss the reality that they are pointing to us. We should see every failure and mistake as a direct warning against the same sinful tendencies in ourselves. The Jewish people are special because of God's promise, but they are typical in their humanity. We aren't told their history so we will judge them. We ought to see from their stories that we deserve judgment.

When we study the Bible, we must remember that it exists to point us to the truth about who God is and who we are in relation to him. We must constantly keep on guard against our tendency to make more of the message than it is. When we make this mistake, we not only put something alongside God, but we build a wall between his will and ours, and we will not easily repent of something we think we have done with the approval of God's very word. Never forget John 5:39-40:

> You diligently study the Scriptures because you think that by them you possess eternal life. These are the Scriptures that testify about me.

DAY 2

Why We Need The Bible: We Aren't Like God

For my thoughts are not your thoughts, neither are your ways my ways," declares the LORD. "As the heavens are higher than the earth, so are my ways higher than your ways and my thoughts than your thoughts. As the rain and the snow come down from heaven, and do not return to it without watering the earth and making it bud and flourish, so that it yields seed for the sower and bread for the eater, so is my word that goes out from my mouth: It will not return to me empty, but will accomplish what I desire and achieve the purpose for which I sent it.

Isaiah 55:8-11

Most Christians steer clear of the book of Isaiah. That's understandable. The prophetic oracles that make up most of the book can be challenging. They're great, but they can be a little advanced because they're written as artistic poetry and require background knowledge.

But for all of that, the messages of these oracles are within our reach, and one of the more well-known ones is Isaiah 55. The strange thing about this chapter is that it has three or four famous pieces, but people rarely see those parts as one connected whole.

For example, when you want to show someone that the Gospel is free, one passage to look to is Isaiah 55:1-2:

Come, all you who are thirsty, come to the waters; and you who have no money, come, buy and eat! Come, buy wine and milk without money and without cost. Why spend money on what is not bread, and your labor on what does not satisfy? Listen, listen to me, and eat what is good, and your soul will delight in the richest of fare [food and drink].

If we want to talk about the importance and power of Scripture, a great passage to quote is Isaiah 55:10-11, which you have just read above. If things happen in our lives that we don't understand, it is not uncommon for someone to quote Isaiah 55:8-9:

> *"For my thoughts are not your thoughts, neither are your ways my ways," declares the LORD. "As the heavens are higher than the earth, so are my ways higher than your ways and my thoughts than your thoughts."*

These uses of each passage are truly fair and proper, but there is something lost when we don't see the message of this chapter as a whole, unified statement. We will see each piece more fully if we see not only their "quote-ability," but also their message as a whole teaching.

The first two verses of the chapter are about God's free and generous invitation, which the Bible calls "grace." He tells the people to come to him and he will accept them, pardon them and bless them if they respond and come. But what are they literally coming to? Verses 3-5 tell us:

> *I will make an everlasting covenant with you, my faithful love promised to David. See, I have made him a witness to the peoples, a leader and commander of the peoples. Surely you will summon nations you know not, and nations that do not know you will hasten to you, because of the LORD your God, the Holy One of Israel, for he has endowed you with splendor.*

King David was long dead by the time this was written, but God promised a second David in the line of kings who would be a confirmation of the covenant he made with the people. This covenant, which is an everlasting commitment, promises that he will bring a second David to form a new nation,[1] one which he will make amazing ("endowed with splendor"). When we look back at Isaiah 54, the chapter just

---

1   The word "nations" in the original language is singular. See the New American Standard translation.

before it, we see it is a nation not based on biology or race but based on God's salvation through the one he would set apart as savior, the Christ. That nation is what we now call the Church.[2]

Then, God goes on to invite all of the wicked and evil people in the world[3] to respond to this invitation to join this new amazing nation in Isaiah 55:6-7:

> Seek the LORD while he may be found; call on him while he is near. Let the wicked forsake his way and the evil man his thoughts. Let him turn to the LORD, and he [the LORD] will have mercy on him, and to our God, for he will freely pardon.

God extends the invitation to the weak and the wicked so long as they come "while he may be found," because this amazingly good and gracious God will "freely pardon" anyone willing to turn from their evil ways and thoughts and come to God for forgiveness.

WE DON'T THINK THIS WAY

It is at *this* point that God says, "For, my thoughts are not your thoughts." What thoughts does he mean? Is this a general statement? No, it is incredibly specific. God is referring to his thoughts on how to redeem a people of God. People, you and I, naturally expect salvation to come to good people like us. This is how we think a respectable and moral God should think and behave. But these are not *God's* thoughts and ways. Salvation would not come to one group of people on the basis of personal moral performance. Rather, it would come to all people who are willing to turn from evil and seek God's forgiveness or his pardon.

Humans don't think this way. It's not like us. It actually offends us. God acknowledges that and tells us we're

---

2   Church capitalized is a reference to the universal Church made up of all who have trusted in God's promise of salvation throughout all peoples, places and times. The lower case church refers to the local church, the local gathering of the universal Church to live out their new identity in Christ in the organization he formed and commanded.

3   This is the "typical humanity" discussed in Day 1.

wrong, but we want to be right. Regardless, God wants to welcome the weak and the wicked into a new amazing nation of joy and peace (see Isaiah 55:12-13).

THE PLAIN THING THAT'S INCOMPREHENSIBLE

Is it just the Jews who got this wrong? 1 Corinthians 2:8-10 gives us some perspective:

> *None of the rulers of this age understood it, for if they had, they would not have crucified the Lord of glory. However, as it is written: "No eye has seen, no ear has heard, no mind has conceived what God has prepared for those who love him" – but God has revealed it to us by his Spirit.*

Did you think this verse is about heaven? It usually gets quoted that way, but look closer. What has God prepared for those who love him? He has prepared the crucified Lord of Glory, Jesus. It happens to be true of heaven, but the verse isn't about heaven. It's about Jesus. Yet I can't tell you how many times I quoted that verse referring to heaven until I saw it this way. The Jews missed it, and we miss it. His ways are higher than our ways.

THINKING THE HIGHER THOUGHTS

So then what are we to do? How can we be expected to believe rightly and respond to God's ways instead of just following our own? How do you follow the ways of God when they are apparently incomprehensible?

Isaiah 55:10-11 answers these questions plainly. We know because God initiates communication to us through his word, which we call revelation. The fact that we would not naturally comprehend God's ways does not mean God cannot teach them to us if we'll read *and* listen. Our greatest need is not for God to affirm our thoughts,

> Our greatest need is not for God to affirm our thoughts, but to tell us his. We do not need our ways affirmed; we need his ways disclosed.

but to tell us his. We do not need our ways affirmed; we need his ways disclosed.

Our need for God to reveal his higher thoughts to us is the foundation of our great need to know the Bible, the written word of God. The Bible is God's revelation of his character and actions, especially in his perfect Word made flesh: the Savior, Jesus Christ. It is no wonder that such a book could be compared to the spring rains that make the countryside bud and grow so well that they not only pro-duce grain for eating, but plenty is left over for planting (Isaiah 55:10).

WHY WE NEED THE BIBLE

The ultimate point of Isaiah 55 is that we are in need of God's word. Since his ways are higher than ours, there can literally be no possible substitute for clear communication from God himself. That communication comes to us in Jesus Christ through the written Bible applied by God's Spirit. We access the knowledge we need of God the Father's will and rule, the work of the Son and the activity of the Holy Spirit in this one precious book.

When we see the Bible this way, it does three things:

1. We are free from treating the Bible superstitiously or reading it as a kind of religious ritual. We realize that it is not a charm that we must read to get a magical blessing or to avoid a curse. We are not commanded to read it every day, and there is no prescribed duty to read any amount. Reading the Bible doesn't get us God's favor.

2. We see the Bible as the needed source of knowledge and wisdom that it is. We begin to understand its value and recognize that if we miss reading it, the loss is ours. We no longer feel an anxious guilt for ignoring the Bible, even if we feel the practical guilt from foolishly neglecting our good and our purpose by neglecting Scripture.

3. We are free to come to the Bible with anticipation and excitement, even while expecting it to offend and contradict us. We know we are about to encounter something very other than ourselves, but we invite rather than resist its correction and discipline. We expect it to be other and higher. We expect God's ways not to be our ways. And we relish the opportunity to hear from God rather than just be affirmed. In the long run, it is much more encouraging, inspiring and transformational.

DAY 3

Reading The Bible For Yourself: Discipline and Tactics

THE GREATEST GOAL AND THE GREATEST TOOL

Becoming a student of the Bible is one of the best investments you can make in your life. We study the Bible to know God and to become more like Christ. This is called godliness. In 1 Timothy 4:8 Paul says, "Physical training is of some value, but godliness has value for all things, holding promise for both the present life and the life to come." His claim is that there is nothing more beneficial in the present or for eternity than becoming more like Jesus. In 2 Timothy 3:16-17 he says,

> All Scripture is God breathed and is useful for teaching, rebuking, correcting and training in righteousness so that [God's people][1] may be thoroughly equipped for every good work.

In this context, "righteousness" means the same thing as godliness. Paul is claiming that godliness has value in everything, and the greatest coach we have in pursuit of it is the Holy Spirit's teaching through the Scriptures.

Therefore, one of the best steps of spiritual growth, and one of the fastest ways to grow spiritually, is to learn to read the Bible for yourself. To do this *you will need a practice that is realistic, habitual and expandable.* These three criteria should be the same for all of us, but there are quite different ways to accomplish them.

REALISTIC AND HABITUAL

There are two main things to focus on if you are just getting started reading the Bible: Do something *realistic* and do

---

1   The NIV translation reads "so that the man of God may be thoroughly equipped for every good work." The Greek word for "man" is the generic word for human (anthropos) not the specific male word (aner).

something *habitual*. Don't try to become a Bible scholar in five weeks. Just because your plate is full doesn't mean you should stuff your mouth. Think long term: set a sustainable and productive yet relaxed pace.

> Godliness has value in everything, and the greatest coach we have in pursuit of it is the Holy Spirit's teaching through the Scriptures.

Start with something realistic. Start with reading the Bible for just five to seven minutes a day. If you already read the Bible, you could try bracketing out a little more time for Bible study or picking a single day each week where you could sit down and read for an hour straight. The key here is to decide to do something that you will really do. This will help you get the discipline[2] started in your life and help you begin to realize the benefits that come from reading God's word.

It has to be realistic, because it has to become habitual. Choose something that you can do on set days each week and preferably every day. I have my Bible reading and prayer time blocked out in my internet calendar so that my staff and my wife can see when I am praying and reading the Bible. You might have to tell your children, "When mommy is sitting at this desk, you don't interrupt me." You might read the Bible out loud two days each week at breakfast with your family for four minutes. You might listen to a Bible app when you're washing the dishes, going for a run or commuting. You could decide that Mondays and Wednesdays you won't watch television between 8:30 and 10:30 PM so that you can attend to the Bible and quality Christian teaching.

The key here is not to let yourself believe that the structure is the purpose. Just as we can mistake the Bible as the main thing, we can mistake our rituals as efficacious on their own. The structure is *an aid* to your willpower and *a*

---

2   Why is discipline necessary if the Bible is so good for us? It's good in the same way exercise is good for us. Its help is a long-run kind of help that never feels urgent. The non-urgent and spiritual things in our lives are the easiest to forget, yet the most important. We need to force ourselves to put them in their right place, usually through rituals, practices and disciplines built into our schedules.

practical application of your convictions. It's the same reason I have a "no ice cream after 8:30 PM" rule. It's because I'm going to want ice cream after 8:30 PM, but I don't want the effects of ice cream that I've eaten after 8:30 PM. I know that at 9:20 PM I'm going to need a rule to aid my willpower and to help me live out the habits that will build the life I want. It's the same reason I have an 8:00 AM prayer rule for Monday, Wednesday and Thursday.

I want to live out my best premeditated convictions and not my worst spontaneous weaknesses.[3] When our disciplines are combined with faith as the reason we do them so that we can become more like Jesus, and not so that we can fulfill a religious duty, they will have the results we seek.

> I want to live out my best premeditated convictions and not my worst spontaneous weaknesses.

PRACTICAL THINGS

There are some obstacles that make even a practical and habitual plan really difficult. Here is some advice to aid in practical and habitual success:

1. **Get a Bible you can read.** Inexpensive Bibles are available, and most churches will gladly give you one. There are great modern English Bible translations,[4] so don't struggle with the King James version just because that's what's in your house. I'd recommend trying the New International Version (NIV) or the English Standard Version (ESV).[5] Both are accurate and readable translations available in trustworthy

---

3   That sentence is what "being myself" should mean but most modern people mean the opposite. That could be a good small group discussion.

4   If you have come across criticisms of the modern English translation that have confused you, talk to your pastor or another trusted Christian about it. There is a lot of misinformation out there, especially on the internet. Most of it is wrong but sounds really compelling.

5   There are editions available with extra information to help you understand background and see how what you're reading fits within the whole story. I recommend the *NIV Study Bible* or the *Life Application Bible* for a New International Version Bible. The *ESV Study Bible* is great for an English Standard Version Bible. Other good English translations are NET, HCSB, NLT and NASB.

study editions.

2. **Have a ritual.** I'd encourage you to build your own little Bible reading ritual. I know that sounds "religious," but it doesn't have to include incense and candles. You probably have some ritual surrounding watching your favorite TV show or sports team. You sit in the same place, with the same people, with the remote in the same spot, in a certain outfit, and so on. It builds excitement, camaraderie and concentration. Make a ritual for studying the Bible. For some people, it's just the same chair and desk at the same time each morning. Some people do it when they have their coffee. Some like to follow the same order each time: pray, read, journal. By having a ritual, you slowly train your body to shift gears and concentrate. Focus is most people's biggest obstacle. A ritual can help.

3. **Have a method.** For quite a while, people have referred to having a "quiet time" or "doing my personal devotions" or "TAG time" (Time Alone with God) as ways of talking about reading the Bible and praying privately outside of church. I've heard college students call it "hanging out with God." Earlier generations (1600s - 1800s) called it "private worship." And if you go back before the printing press, there was a daily service at the church where people could hear the Scriptures read and explained. Christians have long fed on the Bible every day, but how we've done so has changed over time.

Generally speaking, a method for devotions or quiet time normally includes praying and Bible reading. It will often include meditation (trying to think more deeply and contemplatively about the passage read), and sometimes a focus on application. Some people try to bring this all together by journaling. They'll write down what they prayed, what they read and what they believe the proper application should be.

THOUGHTS ABOUT EXPANSION

Once your practice is habitual and realistic, you can expand it over time until you hit a sweet spot. There are a lot of ways to do this. You can slow down and study more deeply. Some people use audio apps and listen to the Bible.[6] I like having a weekly extended reading time where I just read as much as I can without stopping. Ultimately, we hope just to get to the point of enjoying reading the Bible. Once it's a pleasure, expansion happens much more easily. One of my seminary professors once asked our class, "You work with the Bible constantly, but do you LIKE reading it? Do you read it for enriching enjoyment?"

That may sound odd to those starting out. But as you get acquainted with the Bible, you may find that you should and do enjoy reading it. You'll always experience difficulty in learning from Scripture. After all, someone is playing defense (devils), and our pride and fear are allergic to its content. Just remember, the Bible is the greatest tool towards the greatest human end: becoming like Jesus.

---

6   Many Bible scholars have noted that the Bible was written to be heard by an oral reader since it was written at a time before printing and widespread literacy.

DAY 4

Knowing The Bible Together: Studying with the Church

JESUS TAUGHT THE BIBLE

Knowing the Bible is one of the most important endeavors of Christian growth. You can see this in Jesus' disciples. Although Peter and John were not formally educated, after three years, the religious leaders "took note that these men had been with Jesus" (Acts 4:13).

Why did they take note of this?

It's because these Jesus-followers were from a line of ignorant country fishermen, and Peter had just connected Jesus' death and resurrection to an obscure verse in Psalm 118. The religious leaders were astonished at his spiritual and biblical understanding. You can see in all the writings of the apostles that the New Testament was written with a profound and intricate understanding of the meaning of the Old Testament. Sometimes people think Jesus just taught a lot of new things that were completely different from the Old Testament. That's completely false. He claimed that everything he taught was the proper interpretation, application and understanding of the Old Testament (Matthew 5:17). Furthermore, he claimed that every page of the Old Testament, when properly understood, is in some way about him (Luke 24:27).

The importance of learning the Bible should be seen in our church's structure and environments. The most commonly reported reason people give for growing in their faith right after they accept Christ is that they begin to read the Bible for themselves. Yet most people are completely ignorant of the content of the Bible, so even if we want to know it well, many of us are starting from scratch when we come to it. How do we build our skill and ability in reading and understanding the Bible, especially if we have no background in it?

DON'T DO IT ALONE

Individual skills are not always best learned individually. The most reliable and effective way of learning any new skill or discipline is to learn it from someone more advanced in it than yourself. That's precisely why we have teachers, parents, mentors, professors, master artisans, clubs and the like.

One of the things that annoys my wife is that I'm addicted to learning. It leaves a lot of half-done projects around the house, and it also means I spend a lot of time learning things about which I know *nothing*. Sometimes I can't find other people to teach me and I have to teach myself. Recently I took up mycology: growing medicinal and gourmet mushrooms. You can imagine how easy it was to find a local mentor. It took forever for me to grow my first batch. It was tedious learning because I had to read a few hundred pages about mycology be-

> Individual skills are not always best learned individually.

fore I even knew the right *questions* to ask, and then I had no one to ask! That's just what teaching yourself is like. It can be worth it, but it's terribly inefficient.

When I was pastoring in Florida, a guy in the church named Terry asked me if I would be willing to teach him more about reading and understanding the Bible. Terry was a normal guy. He didn't have a college degree. He had a busy life as a sales manager for Pepsi products, a college-level baseball umpire and a dad with a young son at home. I told him that if he would do the homework that I assigned, then I would meet with him once a week to teach him how to interpret the Bible. We did this for about five months. We worked through a book on Bible interpretation,[1] and we worked through a number of Bible passages of different kinds. That is all the biblical training Terry got. He grew dramatically in his faith and started leading a small group.

---

1   The book we used was *How to Read the Bible for all it's Worth* by Gordon Fee and Douglas Stewart. Now I use *Getting the Message* by Daniel Doriani.

A few years later, in addition to his job, Terry was asked to lead a rural church that was without a pastor. All he did was interpret the Bible and teach people on Wednesday nights and Sunday mornings, and the church almost doubled in size in less than a year. When the people were asked what they found so valuable, they said it was his "deep Bible teaching." Terry's only training was some mentoring and then studying the Bible in a way that was realistic, habitual and expandable.

Most people won't lead a church after they get mentored in studying the Bible. But Terry's level of growth didn't come from some kind of abnormal intellectual talent. It came from his choice to be humble and disciplined enough to be taught. Looking back, it took me four years studying by myself (and expending a lot more time and energy) to get to the place which Terry reached in five months of regular mentoring.

CHOOSING TO GROW

There are three ways in which you can engage with the local church and let people help you grow. But in each case, there are criteria that you should be looking for in the helper.

1. WORSHIP AT A CHURCH WITH EXPOSITIONAL PREACHING

Expositional preaching is simply preaching that brings the meaning of the biblical text out and shows you how that is being done. That doesn't mean a church's sermons have to be tedious Bible studies or follow any specific formula. Yet you want the preacher to "show his work" as he goes along so that at each point you can look at the text and respond, "Why didn't I see that?" Over time, you'll become better at seeing what's there. Not only does this defend against false teaching, it allows you to learn in two ways in every sermon. First, you are actually learning what the pastor is preaching about in the particular passage. But secondly, you are also implicitly learning how to do Bible study. You are learning what questions to ask, what kinds of words to pay attention to and how to track either the flow of an argument through a passage or the meaning of the drama in a story. That second thing can produce more in your life than the first thing because it can help you learn from a hundred other passages. Other forms of preaching simply don't give this second, extremely important benefit.

2. TAKE ADVANTAGE OF BIBLE CLASSES AND SMALL GROUPS

To really grow in our ability to understand and apply the Bible, we need to practice. Classes and small groups are contexts for both instruction and practice. They allow for mentoring in group contexts and offer more time to focus on the discipline and practice of Bible study. It may seem uncomfortable or boring to dedicate an evening every week to a small group meeting. You may feel that staying at church a little longer for a regular class isn't worth your three-year-old getting down late for her nap. Yet the learning that will transform your life for the better is almost always practical and repetitive (which can seem boring). It is almost always inconvenient because it prioritizes the important over the urgent. Beyond the direct benefit, though, of investing in understanding the words of God, we also grow richly simply by surrounding ourselves with the type of people who choose to commit to classes and small groups. They often have great wisdom and experience to offer and can be some of the best and most nourishing company you may ever have.

3. GET A ONE-ON-ONE MENTOR, ESPECIALLY IN BIBLE STUDY

There is absolutely nothing as transformative as a one-on-one mentoring relationship with the proper dynamics. And yet, very few people in churches today are looking either to mentor or to be mentored. We are used to efficiency and effectiveness being functions of volume and technology, so one-on-one mentoring seems strange. It is also a shot to our pride. Our mentor will expect us to have a learning posture, and our mentees may not be completely impressed with everything we say. However, the worth of this dynamic holds true. Mentoring is the most effective mechanism for imparting deep biblical spirituality. Godliness requires modeling as well as explanation. Further, in both godliness and biblical understanding, there are lots of very different problems that might need troubleshooting. That troubleshooting needs to be customized. Lastly, understanding and transformation in godliness often requires customized confrontation and encouragement. Without pointed confrontation and the right kind of encouragement, people just don't grow that much. For all these reasons, get a one-on-one mentor, especially in Bible study[2].

> Godliness requires modeling as well as explanation.

It's true that we live in a technological age in which great resources for spiritual growth and Bible study are available online. At our church, we have a leadership blog called *Engage & Equip* (*www.hpcmadison.com*) which is designed to help people connect with the best of those resources. Yet, while technology can replace many things, the impartation of godliness may be the thing least suited for mechanization. It is best passed on in person, tailored and customized through mentoring, and demonstrated week-in and week-out in learning environments and in expositional preaching.

Jesus wants you to know his written word. It's not easy to do alone, and thankfully, he hasn't left you to do it alone. We are filled with his Spirit and surrounded by his body—the Church—for precisely this reason. Growth is a choice. Do something realistic, habitual and expandable. Let Christ use his body to help you.

---

2 Sometimes younger people or those new to the faith can get discouraged trying to find a mentor. Remember three things: 1) It can take time to find someone. Invest in relationships and go to things where you'll be around more seasoned and experienced Christians. 2) Ask for help. Leaders know more people and will have a better chance of knowing someone that might help you. 3) You usually can't get everything from one person. Some people will be great mentors in one or two things, but not everything. You'll probably need to learn from more than one person. I had a half dozen people teach me things I needed in more short-term and focused relationships. I've never had a long-term, formal mentor.

DAY 5

The Application Bias:
Studying The Bible For a Purpose

bi·as ('bīəs) *A prejudice in favor of or against something.*

SO WHAT?!

Not that long ago, I heard about the pastor of another church who does the same thing at the end of all his sermons. He puts out both hands palms up and shrugs his shoulders. The congregation has been trained through years of practice to yell back, "So what?!" I love that. A good biblical sermon isn't about the Bible, but about what the Bible teaches us about God and ourselves. It always has a bias for usefulness, and it should always have an effect on us. Today. Now. You aren't done knowing what the Bible says in any passage until you apply it.

In Day 1 of this week, we talked about how the Bible points to Christ. Today, we'll look at applying this by studying the Bible with a bias for applying Christ to us. Spiritually healthy Bible study and preaching will have an emphasis on God and a bias toward responding to what we learn about God through application (an application bias).

THE "I'M WRONG" BIAS

Before we can consistently live out an application bias, we need to have an "I'm wrong" bias. That is, we need to expect the Bible not to confirm what we already believe. Further, we have to expect our hearts to resist the change that difference demands.

Every human being suffers from what psychologists call "confirmation bias." We like things that confirm what we think, and we're skeptical of things that don't confirm what we already think. Social science studies have shown that even people who think they like to listen to people who disagree with them don't actually like it or do it much in

145

practice. Learning that we are wrong creates a kind of mental pain called "cognitive dissonance." It feels kind of like musical dissonance, when the notes of a song don't work together and sound like nails scratching on a chalkboard. And yet, if you remember from day two, God's ways are not our ways, and his thoughts are not our thoughts.

When we set out to know God better, we should constantly anticipate being told we are wrong (especially where our culture affirms us). We have to have an "I'm wrong" bias if we want to offset our strong, natural confirmation bias. We have to believe the biblical doctrine of depravity: that we are wrong and in rebellion against God, and that we don't want to know it.

> When we set out to know God better, we should constantly anticipate being told we are wrong (especially where our culture affirms us).

FOUR LEVELS OF APPLICATION

Once we have an attitude oriented toward receiving correction (an "I'm wrong" bias) and toward acting on that correction (an application bias), the next thing is to realize that application isn't always an action or a behavior. To say we should have a "bias for application" doesn't mean every time we read the Bible there should be a new thing we need to do. Imagine reading the Bible every day and coming away with something new you need to do, 365 days a year, for the rest of your life. Sound realistic? Yet you can walk away with an application from the Bible every day without going crazy. *You just have to think about application as broader than behavior.*

In a seminar version of his book, *Getting the Message*, Daniel Doriani talks about four levels of application:

1. What should I do?

Some applications *will* be actions. The Gospel will change our behavior. You should ask, "What am I doing wrong or right, and how should I change my behavior? What is the moral and behavioral implication of this passage? How would I obey it in action?" This is an important set of questions, but it is not the only set.

2. Who should I be?

Some applications will point to identity, wisdom and character rather than just behavior. Virtuous and faithful behavior comes reliably from a heart, will and mind of character. If the Bible passage points to the goodness of contentment or thankfulness, what will the application be? You may need to apply the message not just to how you will act content or thankful, but to how you need to rethink how you think and feel about things in order to form a more naturally thankful and contented character. The central questions is: "Who is God calling me to become?" If you focus on #2, it's hard to go wrong on #1.

3. How can we do this together?

The first two levels are primarily individual in nature. But you are not *only* an individual. Some truths or commands have to be worked out in a community of people, like our family or the church. For example, why do we do church the way we do? Hopefully as this book unfolds, you are seeing that everything we do together as a church is a response to a biblical truth about the Gospel and following Jesus. All of these applications are group applications. We figure them out together, and we live them out together. Make sure you ask yourself (or those you lead) questions that include the word "we."

4. How can I see?

Romans 12:2 says that following Jesus includes losing our conformity with the world and being transformed through a renewing of our mind—of how we think about things. 2 Corinthians 10:5 says that we should "take captive every thought to make it obedient to Christ." God is the Creator of everything, and our thoughts are often bound up in rebellion against his truth. Our heads are like a country full of wild rebels.

Jesus needs to reteach us most of what we think we know about the world. We need to see things like he sees them, as they truly are, and that means we need a new vision of our world. Many passages in the Bible are there to help renew our minds, to change our thinking, feelings and motivations about much of life. Ask regularly: "What way of seeing something does this challenge? How is God challenging me to see it differently?"

A PRODUCTIVE PAIN

Seeking to apply the Bible's message to your life isn't a comfortable experience. It's painful to experience cognitive dissonance. It's difficult to accept change in our behavior, character, relationships and thinking. However, it is a productive pain. It's the feeling of healing. It's the soreness that comes from the building of strength in your soul and character. In order to regularly experience this, you will need to:

1. Go to the Bible regularly with expectation and dependence upon the Holy Spirit

2. Have a bias for application and admitting you're wrong

3. Apply its message on more levels than just behavior

Those simple steps can transform the effect studying the Bible has on you, and God will use them to transform you.

CHOOSE A NEXT STEP

1. Decide that you are going to be a Bible student.

2. Make plans to constantly remember the why: the God you are seeking whom you are not like, and your desire to love and be more like him.

3. Start to read the Bible, however little, with the goal of understanding and obeying God and the expectation that you will be confronted.

4. Study the Bible with someone further along than you. And then soon, study with someone not as far along as you.

SERVE

WEEK 5
SERVE
THE CITY

Jesus was prone to tell his people to love those whom it felt unnatural to love. He tasked them with loving their enemies, doing good to those who hated them, blessing those who cursed them and praying for people who mistreated them (Luke 6:27). He told them to invite people with mental and physical disabilities to their dinner parties (Luke 14:13) and to treat people in hated government positions and parasitic professions like prostitution with dignity. He said it was because that's the only way we can be like him and have a real impact on those around us.

Love always costs something. Sacrificial service is the price of godly influence. We will never melt the hearts of our neighbors if we don't have any warmth toward them. But we must remember that love isn't a cold strategy or manipulative ideology. These neighbors are people, not objects to be won. We must also remember that compassion is not a heart response prompted at a distance. Love always costs something, and one of those costs is always proximity. Heart change requires contact for them and for us. The two constant components in all acts of obedient love are sacrificial service and real personal contact. When both of these are present in doing God's will, we will begin to understand some of the reasons he instructs us to function this way. Obedience is the price of understanding, especially in the dynamics of faith, hope and love. Focusing us on these simple truths and letting them have their effect on us in practice is part of God's blueprint for an unstuck and uncluttered life.

> Sacrificial service is the price of godly influence.

SERVE
THE CITY

SERMON NOTES

WEEK 5
SERVE
THE CITY
SMALL GROUP
DISCUSSION QUESTIONS

WATCH THE SMALL GROUP VIDEO

1. Sacrificial service is the price of influence. How is this statement true or false?

   a. Can you tell a story about a time when you saw this happen?

   b. Can you think of a Bible passage built around this principle?

2. Heart change requires contact.

   a. Give examples from the Bible or from experience of how getting to know someone–and being with them as you served them–impacted them and you more than if the process wasn't personal.

   b. Marvin Olasky, in *The Tragedy of American Compassion,*[1] states that in the early centuries of America, charity was delivered directly from one person to another. The benefits of this were:

      a. The ability to distinguish between real need and false need.

      b. A motivating effect on the recipient *and* the giver.

---

1   Marvin Olasky, *The Tragedy of American Compassion* (Washington, D.C.: Regnery Gateway, 1992).

    c. More givers understanding firsthand the plight of those in need.

    d. A greater sense as to whether what was being done was working.

    e. Less suspicion and judgment between the poorer and richer classes.

How can or should these principles help us to form our service programs in the local church?

3. Obedience is the price of understanding.

    a. What's one task or truth that you only came to understand through experience?

    b. Why is that the case? Why can we accept some things through explanation, while others need to be experienced?

    c. Exercise: Name something that can be described in words and be understood (example: how lying breaks people's ability to trust you). Now name something that you can't easily pass on through a description (example: how to tie a tie).

4. On a scale of 1-10, how committed are you to the idea that Christian growth requires regular sacrificial service? Why?

5. To parents: How does your view of parenting affect your views and actions related to service? What does your child's calendar tell you about your parenting priorities?

RELEVANT SCRIPTURES TO DISCUSS

Luke 14:12-14; John 7:17; Galatians 5:13

DAY 1

Living Distinct and Dispersed

This is what the LORD Almighty, the God of Israel, says to all those I carried into exile from Jerusalem to Babylon: "Build houses and settle down; plant gardens and eat what they produce. Marry and have sons and daughters; find wives for your sons and give your daughters in marriage, so that they too may have sons and daughters. Increase in number there; do not decrease. Also, seek the peace and prosperity of the city to which I have carried you into exile. Pray to the LORD for it, because if it prospers, you too will prosper.

Jeremiah 29:4-7

Jeremiah said, "The word of the LORD came to me: Hanamel son of Shallum your uncle is going to come to you and say, 'Buy my field at Anathoth, because as nearest relative it is your right and duty to buy it.' Then, just as the LORD had said, my cousin Hanamel came to me in the courtyard of the guard and said, 'Buy my field at Anathoth in the territory of Benjamin. Since it is your right to redeem it and possess it, buy it for yourself.' I knew that this was the word of the LORD; so I bought the field.

Jeremiah 32:6-9

GROWING ROOTS

It can be hard making a life in a place that isn't your home. It is your home, but in another way it isn't. It's your home *for now*. I have been living this way since I was 18. I left for college for four years. It was my home, but I knew it wasn't permanent. Then I went to graduate school in Chicago for three years, and it was the same. After that, I pastored in the South for seven years, but I knew we wouldn't stay there forever. And now I've been in Madison for four years.

Fifty years ago, people didn't move around nearly as much as we do now. Something has been lost in all our migrations—a sense of rootedness. It has always been part of God's ultimate promise that we would have an *eternal* rootedness. His promise has always been to give us a home.

On some level, every Christian should feel this tension between the desire for rootedness and a realization that we are not really home. We are citizens of a home we have not visited and yet still long for. Like the children of immigrants reared on the stories of homes in the old country, we look forward to our home in a new country that Jesus told us about. We talk about our home while we are wanderers in the world.

This sense of un-rooted rootedness has always been a mark of God's people. He chose a wanderer in Abraham. Shepherding peoples have always been nomads, and that's what the Hebrews were. Then they were slaves in Egypt, and then they were brought out to wander. They had some rest in the land under their own kings, but then they were exiled from their home and were scattered among the nations.

Many Christians think of the present Church as God's mystical Israel, his holy nation. They tend to relate to the picture of Israel settled in the homeland. Yet that is not the image that the New Testament authors used for the Church. 1 Peter starts this way: "Peter, an apostle of Jesus Christ, to God's elect, strangers in the world, scattered throughout Pontus, Galatia, Cappadocia, Asia and Bithynia" (1 Peter 1:1).

Notice the three descriptors:

1. **The Elect:** This is not a random group of people, but God's chosen ones.

2. **Exiles:** "Strangers" is the New Testament word for sojourner, refugee or exile, a foreigner forced out of his home looking for a temporary home.

3. **Scattered:** Scattered is the opposite of gathered and

refers to this dispersion of Christians as a minority among all the people of the secular world.

The apostle is reminding us in the very first verse of his letter that there is nothing random or heartless about our being scattered in the world. We are God's very elect; he has chosen us and not forgotten us, yet we are exiles and foreigners in countries that can never really be our home. We are scattered among the world in a great dispersion without a country of our own.

The point here is that our present life is less like the residence of the Jews in Israel and much more like the exile of the Jews when they were in Babylon. We are exiles. We are foreigners who are making our home in a place that is not our real home. This fact defines our present identity much more than most Christians realize.

God's vision for living in this kind of context is laid out clearly in the book of Jeremiah. In it, God has sent his people into exile for seventy years. The emphasis on seventy years is that virtually everybody sent into exile will die there. The people Jeremiah was talking to were people who were not going to go home in this life. In that sense, they were exactly like us. Or better, we're exactly like them.

LIVING DISPERSED AND DISTINCT

When any minority group finds itself surrounded by a majority with notably different habits and values, one of two things typically happens. They will either disperse among the majority and assimilate, or they will gather together and separate themselves from the surrounding majority. If they seek to be dispersed and gain the benefits of being in the majority culture, they will virtually always lose their distinct identity and take on the identity of the majority in one or two generations. If they isolate themselves, they begin to lose their engagement with the culture around them. God instructs his people to do neither of these. He instructs them to be dispersed in the city among the majority of the Babylonians and yet to retain their spiritual, moral and cultural identity as God's people. *He calls them to be both dispersed and distinct.* This is his vision for his exiles both past and present.

God gives two main instructions to his people in Jeremiah 29:4-7. First, they must make a home, a real home that maintains their identity as a minority in the secular city. He tells them to buy homes and farms. He tells them to give their sons and daughters in marriage to one another to build families with their distinct spiritual identity. Second, they must increase in number as a distinct people within the city. They were to retain their essential distinction even in their dispersion.

> Distinctly Christian families and churches should be a huge priority for us, especially because we exist as a dispersed minority.

Christians today live with the same expectation. We are supposed to build up the distinct identity we have in Christ. The Church should have our attention, receive our resources and be built up by our hands. We should seek to form families, have children even in a troubled world and increase, not decrease, in the city in which we live. Distinctly Christian families and churches should be a huge priority for us, especially because we exist as a dispersed minority. We need to focus on and emphasize these things to thrive in our distinctness.

FOREIGNERS THAT ARE BETTER THAN CITIZENS

Yet God does not give us the right to set up a separated ghetto. We are not called to have our own gated neighborhoods but to "seek the peace and prosperity of the city to which I have carried you into exile... because if it prospers, you too will prosper" (Jeremiah 29:7). There are two important realities in this command. First, the very city in which we are exiled is chosen by God. He says it is the city "to which *I have carried you* into exile." Our exile is a divine action with a particular intent. The Jewish people were exiled in an act of discipline, but they were also a gift for the peace and prosperity of the city of Babylon.

Similarly, even though we can't know exactly what

trouble in our lives may be due to the discipline of God, we can know that the exile is for our good and for the good of the people among whom we have been dispersed. God's sovereignty and providence has placed us where we are. From his perspective, our neighbors are not random.

Furthermore, God has intentionally tied the fates of the two peoples together. Cities decline and prosper together. Their systems and crime rates–their successes and failures– are not the product of a single person, subculture, or political party. As people are bound together, they are bound to affect each other, which is the heart of why God intends for us to be both dispersed and distinct. We can't affect others if we don't interact with them, and we can't affect them positively if we don't remain distinct. Only by being truly distinct as a gospel-centered, Jesus-imitating people who exult in the glory of God can we deeply and powerfully affect the people among whom God has intentionally dispersed us.

ROOTED IN HOPE

There is one more powerful lesson God taught to Jeremiah that we can never forget. Just before the city of Jerusalem was destroyed, God told Jeremiah to buy a field (see Jeremiah 32:6-9 above). God had said that all of these fields would be destroyed. Jeremiah knew better than anyone that the land would become completely desolate. But God tells Jeremiah, "I want you to buy some of it. I want you to buy a field." To farm is to have hope. To buy real estate in a city burning to the ground is to trust in the promise of a future deferred.

That is why, in my first autumn in Madison, I planted four fruit trees. I knew that I wouldn't get fruit from them for at least five years, and that was the whole point. I had come here to put down roots and to hope in the future for God's people in this city and for this city at large, even though it could never be our true and greater home. But that's nothing like the commitment that Jeremiah made. He bought a field he knew he would never plant. He tells his scribe to take the deed to the field and put it in something sturdy, because someday someone would come back and plant that field.

In this way, you must never, ever, *ever* forget that if you are a Christian, you are an exile, an alien, a refugee and a foreigner. The difference is that you haven't fled your country; you just haven't reached it yet. The place you live is the place in which you have been dispersed to be distinct. God has placed you among secular or pagan people to live like an ambassador of your true home (2 Corinthians 5:20), working intently for their peace and prosperity. Doing so strengthens us immeasurably and can be a great good for all people among whom we live. This place is our home, and yet it isn't. It is our context, but not our identity. It is *where* we are, but we live in it best when we don't mistake it for *who* we are.

FOR FURTHER READING

1 Corinthians 7:29-31

Colossians 3:1-11

1 Timothy 6:17-19

Hebrews 11:8-16

DAY 2

Living Persuasively: Purity With Presence

READ MATTHEW 5:1-16

You are the salt of the earth. But if the salt loses its saltiness, how can it be made salty again? It is no longer good for anything, except to be thrown out and trampled by men. You are the light of the world. A city on a hill cannot be hidden. Neither do people light a lamp and put it under a bowl. Instead they put it on its stand, and it gives light to everyone in the house. In the same way, let your light shine before men, that they may see your good deeds and praise your Father in heaven.

Matthew 5:13-16

BEING LIGHT

What does it mean to be a city on a hill or a lamp that can't be hidden? Jerusalem and other cities in that part of the world were built on top of some kind of hill to be more defensible. Just as they could see people coming a long way off, so they could be seen from a long way off. The main thing about a city on a hill was its visibility and its ability to dominate a landscape. The same thing is true of ancient clay lamps. They usually only had one small flame, which gave the light of a modern candle. Because of this, they were usually set up high so they could give light to a whole room.

That is the point of everything in this passage of Scripture. It is against their nature to be hidden or separated from the surrounding world. A city can't be hidden. Salt must be mixed with something to be of any use. A lamp is meant to shine its light around the room it was lit to illuminate.

The point of this message in Matthew 5 is clear. We are supposed to be Matthew 5:1-12 (the Beatitudes) kind of people in a Matthew 5:13-16 (city on a hill) kind of way. If we try to be holy without being visible, we will be useless since humility, compassion, meekness, a hunger for righteousness, mercy, purity, peacemaking and truth-telling are all social virtues that must happen out in the city. If they are only done in a hidden tribe, what good are they as light? It's like hiding a lamp under a basket or trying to hide a city that's located on a hilltop.

OBVIOUS BUT NOT NATURAL

Now, although this seems like a plain and obvious point, there is a reason Jesus must teach it and a reason Matthew was led to put it in such a prominent place in his Gospel. This is not what people do in the natural course of life. People don't naturally intermingle. They gravitate toward people similar to them. We find comfort in smaller and more predictable groups of people who share our interests and values.

The result of this is what has sometimes been called a "sub-culture," and Christians are very adept at making sub-cultures. In fact, when someone who is not a Christian becomes a Christian, it often takes less than two years for them to have only Christian friends, especially close friends.[1] In seminary, I learned that more than 90% of Christians have never led anyone to faith. It's because they do not have a meaningful relationship with anyone *outside* of the faith. It is important for us to accept that creating a sealed sub-culture is what will happen if we do nothing intentionally to stop it. It is the natural movement of all like-minded people, and it is what every church will become unless it deliberately and consistently forces itself to be something else.

The solution to this is not to become just like our culture. There are some Christians who don't seem interested in the

---

1   I'm not claiming that this is necessarily wrong. Close friendship comes out of a shared journey, shared interests and shared values. When we come to follow Jesus, he reorders our interests and completely rearranges our values. The natural pull of this is to seek deep spiritual friendships with people seeking to follow Jesus and to grow in godliness. Non-Christians aren't always good candidates for this, so we gravitate toward Christians until they're the only people in our orbit.

family of God and seem to spend all of their time and energy being as much like the culture as possible. But *worldliness is just as ineffective as withdrawal.* It is like putting a lamp on a stand and then not lighting it. Further, the "you" of Matthew 5 is plural. Jesus is speaking to a group—to a church—that he's encouraging to be a culture within a culture, a city within the city, distinct and yet visible.

So, if we are neither to be just like the culture, nor separate from it, what's the alternative? I think the picture Jesus gives in Matthew 5 is that of a counter-culture, except without the arrogance and defensiveness that counter-cultures usually have towards mainstream society. A counter-culture is a group of people who are distinguished from the culture but are fully engaged within the culture. They are not like the rest of the city, but everyone knows that they are a full part of the city, and they love the people in it as their own, both correcting the culture and sacrificing for its good, peace and prosperity.

LIVING PERSUASIVELY

Living persuasively as a group requires at least three things: we need a high level of spiritual potency in a significant majority of us, we need to live among the city's people and we need someone to speak clearly and persuasively to help spiritual outsiders rightly interpret what they are experiencing. One course on evangelism put it into an equation like this:

HIGH POTENCY + CLOSE PROXIMITY + CLEAR

COMMUNICATION =

MAXIMUM IMPACT[2]

Thinking in terms of high potency can be clearer than thinking that we have to "be different." Some Christians seem to like to be different by being weird or strange. It's

---

2 Bill Hybels and Mark Mittleberg, *Becoming a Contagious Christian* (Grand Rapids, MI: Zondervan, 1994), 47.

kind of like when junior high girls try to get noticed by being dramatic rather than by living the drama of doing something important. It just feels manufactured and hollow to everyone around them. High potency is simply profound godliness in heart, mind, speech and action. The more unnecessarily weird or strange we are in that potency, the less effective its impact. It is okay to be normal. What we want to avoid is being typical. Simply making virtuous decisions on the basis of character and faith will make us atypical enough for people to notice, even if it takes a little time.

> It is okay to be normal. What we want to avoid is being typical.

OPENING YOUR MOUTH

It has always bothered me that people attribute this quote to St. Francis of Assisi: "Preach the Gospel always, use words if necessary." There is no evidence that St. Francis ever said that. In fact, the legends of St. Francis talk about him preaching the Gospel out in the woods to animals and birds. He did not believe in a division between words and action. He preached the Gospel effectively because he believed in absolute unity between our words and our actions.

It is wrong to talk about the Gospel without living the Gospel. However, the opposite is also true. It is both wrong and nonsensical to live the gospel and not talk about it. We can't assume that when people experience Christian love and sacrificial service they will intuitively interpret it properly and come to Christ. Without speech, we leave people to interpret our actions in any way that occurs to them or in any way other people tell them to. There is no encouragement anywhere in the Bible to show the Gospel and not speak it. *Our God is a showing and speaking God.* We would not have known him without his actions, but we could not have understood his actions had he not seen fit to speak. He has given us "the message of reconciliation" (2 Corinthians 5:19) in the form of the Good News. Messages and news are not so much *shown* as they are *told.*

Remember, for most of us, we can feel a social and

cultural pressure to shut up about Jesus. Our situation requires wisdom. We must work hard to clarify what we're saying and to say it in a way that will be the least offensive and most persuasive for the hearer. But faithfulness requires speech nonetheless. It can be through declaration, and it can also be through invitation to an environment where that declaration will happen best (like a church or small group).

CLOSE PROXIMITY OF FRIENDSHIP

All of this works only in the form of direct relationships. We have to have close relational proximity to people. People aren't personally transformed by "services" provided by an impersonal system or institutional bureaucracy. People are personally transformed when someone who doesn't have to serves them sacrificially, and they understand why through compelling action and persuasive communication.

It's the same reason that "ministries" work only as well as the people who do them. At our church, we call our ministries "environments" because we don't want people to think that they're ends in themselves. They aren't something, they are environments *for* something. They're environments in which we serve and speak. They're places to form real friendships. They are places where people can experience high potency, enjoy the close proximity and consider the clearly communicated message of Jesus.

FOR FURTHER REFLECTION

1. How long have you been a Christian?

2. Are you connected to anyone outside of the sub-culture?

3. Do you see your Christian community more as a safe sub-culture or as an engaged counter-culture?

4. Of the three parts to living persuasively, which are you strongest in? Which are you weakest in? How can the church be a place to use your strength or encourage you in your weakness?

You can read more on "Purity and Presence" in Appendix 8.

DAY 3
The Gospel and Our Neighbor

Love your neighbor as yourself.   Leviticus 19:18

"Which of these three do you think was a neighbor to the man who fell into the hands of robbers?" The expert in the law replied, "The one who had mercy on him." Jesus told him, "Go and do likewise."
Luke 10:36-37

WHAT DOES IT MEAN TO LOVE GOD?

"Love your neighbor as yourself" is one of the most well-known commands in the Bible (quoted 10 times in the New Testament[1]). In all of the first three Gospels, an episode is recorded in which Jesus is asked which law is the most important. Jesus affirms that the summary of all the Old Testament law is to love God and to love our neighbors. In Matthew 22:40 he even says, "All the Law and the Prophets," that is, the whole Bible up to that point, "hang on these two commands." Have you ever wondered why Jesus couldn't just answer the question? The guy did clearly ask him what the *one* greatest commandment was. Why did he need to answer with two?

I think God knew that we needed to hear two parts to this in order to understand what it really demands of us. First, we are to love God with everything we've got. Got it? Ready? Ok. How are you going to practically do that? That could mean *anything* (which is confusing) or it could mean *everything* (which is discouraging). Do you see the problem?

If Jesus had simply told people to love God, they might have picked and chosen their way through the law or their

---

1   Also quoted in Matthew 5:43, 19:19, 22:39; Mark 12:31, 12:33; Luke 10:27; Romans 13:9; Galatians 5:14; and James 2:8.

169

imaginations, and they probably would have picked all of the easiest stuff.[2] I think Jesus knew that if he was going to tell people that loving God was the most important thing in the world, he was going to have to give us concrete direction on how to do that.

There are certainly some ways we love God that have little to do with our neighbors. There are some biblical acts of direct worship. However, the one summary Jesus gives us of all of God's instructions is focused on the one thing we are perhaps most prone to avoid: our neighbor.[3]

In fact, in other places, God teaches that even our acts of direct worship are only as valid as our concrete obedience of loving people. God cannot stomach any profession of love for him that is not in harmony with an authentic love for his image bearers in our midst (1 Samuel 15:22; Isaiah 1:10-19; Matthew 5:23-24; James 3:9).

But who is our neighbor?

THE CITY IS OUR NEIGHBOR

Leviticus 19:18 (quoted at the beginning of today's reading) is quoted in three places in the New Testament's letters. These passages challenge even further our neglect of our neighbors. They show us that we are most likely to forget about our poor and non-Christian neighbors in favor of *religious substitutes.*

This command to love our neighbor first shows up in Romans 13:9. This is an important chapter because it discusses the Christian's relationship to civil authorities and to our non-Christian neighbors. The passage tells us to obey the government, including paying our taxes and fees, and

---

2   In a number of places in the Old Testament, God is angry with the people because they do the easy stuff, like the religious rituals and sacrifices, and then they are terrible to each other. Doing rituals is easier than being loving, good and holy toward real people.

3   The primacy of our neighbor could be pushed further when God said to Saul, "To obey is better than sacrifice and to heed better than the fat of rams" (1 Samuel 15:22). This is because, when it comes to valuing and loving God, obedience has primacy over acts of worship that can be offered instead of obedience. Obedience must be present for worship to be valid and loving. Most of God's commands that we are meant to obey concern our neighbors.

to show respect to our civil officials. We are told that we do this not only because it's required, but because it's right.

Paul goes on to say that we must pay our taxes because we should not allow any debt to be outstanding except the one we can never pay off: the debt of love. He concludes his discussion of the law with: "Whatever other commandments there may be are summed up in this one rule: Love your neighbor as yourself. Love does no harm to its neighbor. Therefore love is the fulfillment of the law" (Romans 13:9b). *Context* is important here. Who is our neighbor in this passage? Our civil society is our neighbor. That means our city and even our nation must be treated as our neighborhood on some level. We cannot just love the people in our church or the people of our political party; we have to love the people of our city and society.

THE POOR ARE OUR NEIGHBOR

Within this broad neighborhood, we are particularly prone to treat one group of people as though they must be someone else's neighbor: the poor and weak. James, the brother of Jesus, calls the neighbor commandment the "royal law." In chapter two of the book of James, he discusses our tendency to treat wealthy, well-dressed and important people better than poor-looking and shabby people. It is a natural enough tendency, but James says this about it:

> *Have you not discriminated among yourselves and become judges with evil thoughts?...If you really keep the royal law found in Scripture, "Love your neighbor as yourself," you are doing right. But if you show favoritism, you sin and are convicted by the law as lawbreakers.*
>
> James 2:8-9

Ouch! In fact, all of chapter two is written against our instinct to show favoritism. James says that just as we can love our neighbor and keep the whole law, this also means that when we overlook our poor neighbor we break the whole law. The summary of all things into one thing cuts both ways. The minute two people come into our church and we treat one better than the other, we show that we do not live by the impartial Gospel. *We show that it is something other than God's image and Christ's death that makes someone valuable to us. We show that what we really value is the thing we favor, whether it is the person's power, wealth, reputation, or attractiveness.*

This is precisely why many passages of Scripture tell us that how we treat the poor is the clearest indication of what we think of God[4] and why Jesus can credit what we do to the poor as what we do to him (Matthew 25:31-46). These verses in Romans 13 and James 2 are meant to force us to face our tendency to neglect our city and the poor to favor people like ourselves who have something to offer us.

OUR NEIGHBOR ISN'T GOD

The third appearance of this instruction is in Galatians 5:14. This passage comes at the end of a very different discussion. The apostle Paul is telling us that we are free from the law, and we should not be trying to earn God's favor by following it. To do so is to abandon the Gospel and to turn back to religion. This is precisely why Jesus did not say that the greatest commandment was to love your neighbor as yourself. He said it was to love God. He knew that anyone who has truly come to love God as vigorously as they once loved themselves would have love that needed to pour out onto something. That something was to be our neighbors.

Paul forces this proper order back on us. He knows that this one law, if treated as a religion, would be a hundred times more oppressive than the first law could have ever been. He says,

> *You, my brothers, were called to be free. But do not use your freedom to indulge the sinful nature; rather, serve one another in love. The entire law is summed up in a single command: "Love your neighbor as*

---

4 Because all they have to commend themselves to us is the image of God, they prove how big of a difference God's image makes to us. Examples: Proverbs 17:5, 14:21, 14:31; 1 John 3:17.

yourself"...So I say, live by the Spirit.

Galatians 5:13-14, 16

You see, it is so easy to turn this back into a religion of effort. It's easy to twist this into "If you love your neighbor, then you are loving God, and if you love God, God will love you." That is moralism, which can quickly become dead, destructive legalism.

What the apostle and the Spirit are pleading for is that we believe the Gospel that says we are radically loved and accepted by God in Jesus Christ. We must be filled with a new love empowered by the Holy Spirit so that we want to love God with everything we've got. But we have to practically and physically pour that love out on someone we can see, feel and touch: our neighbor.

The more that love resembles the love Jesus gave us, the more it will seek out those who *need* that love instead of people who can *repay* that love. We will seek those far from God, those in the general society and those in need. We will not do it to impress God but because of what God has impressed upon us in Christ. Only then, in the freedom of the Gospel, will we fulfill the whole of the perfect law.

DAY 4

Service In The Suburbs: Transforming Our Thinking

LIFE IN THE 'BURBS

Not everyone who reads this will identify with the suburban lifestyle. But my context of ministry is in the city of Madison, Wisconsin. Madison is a true city with a population of 240,000 and a metro population of 568,000, ranking 82nd in the United States.[1] But in another sense, it is an amalgamation of suburbs and neighborhoods sprawling across a county. The dynamics of most of these neighborhoods tend to follow that of suburbs.

Although suburbs can be demonized, more and more people still want to live in them. In 1998 the ten largest cities had the same combined population as they had in 1950. Yet the suburbs doubled in size from 1900 to 1950, and again from 1950 to 2000, making up about 52% of the American population.[2] *The suburbs are the majority, and evangelical Christians have moved into them at a higher proportion than almost anyone else.*

The reason is that the suburbs provide a good life. People like them. Suburban life offers four main benefits that can also become obstacles to a serving lifestyle:

1. **Value:** We have real space in square footage, basements, yards and parks.

2. **Privacy and Control:** We can control our surroundings and close our garage doors.

3. **Opportunities:** We have opportunities for good jobs, good schools and like-minded neighbors.

---

1   City-data.com, "Top 100 biggest cities," http://www.city-data.com/top1.html (accessed 15 Jul. 2014).

2   Theodore Caplow, Louis Hicks and Ben J. Wattenberg, The First Measured Century: An Illustrated Guide to Trends in America, 1900-2000 (Washington, D.C.: American Enterprise Institute Press, 2000), http://www.pbs.org/fmc/book/1population6.htm (accessed 15 Jul. 2014).

4. Safety and Security: We have a separation from urban problems, especially violent crime, vandalism, overt drug use and theft.

The suburbs provide proximity to the benefits of the city and the country while being separate from the inherent problems of concentration or isolation. But suburban life in the 1950s or even the 1980s was different than it is today. In those days, kids used to come home on their bikes when the streetlights came on, and they played with the same friends every day. Suburban life has dramatically changed in its dynamics, its expenses and its technologies.

Suburban life has higher fixed costs, which affects generosity. It has intense social pressures to conform to sometimes controlling values exemplified in neighborhood association covenants.[3] There is a very specific and intense set of views about children and how they should be nurtured and given "every advantage."

Suburban life also self-sorts—separates us from people and things we don't want to be around—and it tends to over-sort. When the suburbs separate us from crime centers, they also tend to separate us from other classes (and often races and nationalities) of people through economic segregation.[4] The product of this can be a narrower life experience and a bubble mentality.[5]

Further, many educated suburbanites know how little effect aid programs have had on those in need, which can kill our motivation further. The two wars America can't seem to win are the war on poverty (1964-?) and the war on

---

3   Some of these can seem minor, but inordinate amounts of money and time can be spent keeping your house looking nice enough. There can also be social pressures about allowing too many people to live with you or having too many guests parking on the street too often. An open and hospitable lifestyle can produce tension with suburban neighbors seeking control and privacy.

4   One of my greatest disappointments in living in Chicago was how segregated the city was. This was not because housing segregation was legal, but because the cost of housing segregated the city by class. In an age of equal rights, many modern cities and suburbs are still profoundly segregated.

5   When you add the self-sorting properties of technology, separation and segregation become even more profound.

drugs (1971-?). Fifty years and $21 trillion later, the poverty rate hasn't budged. The realities of modern social problems and our empirical inability to significantly change them can cast a mist over even the clearest moral vision. It's terribly demotivating. Why sacrifice deeply for something you apparently can't change physically or spiritually? Even Jesus said that the poor would always be with us and that the majority of people wouldn't listen to his message. So, why fight a long defeat?

In light of all this, when suburbanite Christians are challenged to engage in sacrificial service and to do so as a lifestyle with their children, it can seem like an attack on a lifestyle they have specifically chosen for positive and sensible reasons, and it can all seem to be in service to a futile initiative.

THE DANGERS OF CAMELOT

In any culture, the Christian seeking the mind of Christ must decide what to *receive* as it is, *reject* outright or somehow *redeem* in light of the Gospel.[6]

Christian theologians call this process "disenculturation and theological integration."[7] Disenculturation is the process of losing our *destructive* cultural blinders that are part of secular culture without putting on *protective* religious and legalistic blinders. That's the negative. Positively, we have to integrate what we believe about God with how we see the world. Some people call this integration "forming a Christian worldview." Whatever we call it, we have to think clearly about the suburbs and what in them we can receive,

> I believe the three biggest dangers we have to face are how we love our privacy, leisure and children.

---

6   Mark Driscoll, "Why Christians Go Postal over Facebook, Jay-Z, Yoga, Avatar, and Culture in General," The Resurgence, Resurgence, http://theresurgence.com/2010/12/07/why-christians-go-postal-over-facebook-jay-z-yoga-avatar-and-culture-in-general (accessed 15 Jul. 2014).

7   Lovelace, *Dynamics*, 396-400.

should reject and might redeem. I believe the three biggest dangers we have to face are how we love our privacy, leisure and children.

REDEEMING THE 'BURBS

One of the reasons we find it very difficult to serve other people sacrificially is that we think about it organizationally instead of organically. We think of it as an added demand on our time and as something that happens in another place. But what if we didn't? What if we saw our own kitchen table as our place of service? What if we saw the home as a counter-kingdom where people can experience a place where Jesus is King over all things? And why shouldn't these things be included in something we already do, like dinner? This is part of the genius of the small group, but the small group is only one application of the virtue of hospitality and is an expression of the greater intergenerational genius called family.

It's true that incorporating the love of others into our normal lives will impact our privacy and our leisure. Yet much of the leisure into which we cannot include others may not be very good for us anyway. The latest numbers say that the average American is watching more than twenty-five hours of television per week.[8] Add to this another three hours with online devices, and it becomes obvious why we don't have time for the real world. We're living in a virtual one. The best way to stop these habits is to replace them with something better, like hospitality and service.

THE HIDDEN PROBLEM

I know this will be controversial for some readers, but I believe a critical part of the problem is our view of children. After all, many urbanites call the 'burbs the "land of the breeders." *Pop and politicized psychology and basic economics have radically changed the way we view children.* We've been taught that kids are enormously fragile, must come first in

---

8   According to Nielsen statistics, many seniors are now averaging nearly seven hours per day, and 67% of Americans watch television while eating dinner.

every way in our lives, require enormous amounts of quality time, and (because their self-esteem is their most important trait) should be positively nurtured, not negatively disciplined. This is mostly all false both biblically and scientifically,[9] yet is almost universally believed, especially in American churches.

Basic economic observation shows us that the lifestyle of professionals is embattled. College entrance is getting more difficult and expensive, while professionals are working longer for less. Parents realize that an increasing number of suburban children will be in head-to-head competition with themselves and others in a shrinking pool of jobs that are getting progressively mechanized and exported.

This has led to something of a frenzy in three areas of parenting: nurture, competition and protection.[10] It's an arms race being fought by soccer moms and power dads in the midst of emotionally deafening peer pressure and cultural expectations. It's like a Cold War in the American middle classes. Parents may struggle to describe this, but most of the parents I know feel it, hate it and feel bullied by it.

Yet biblical Christians should be able to sniff out the problem with this. The fragility of children is a self-fulfilling prophecy. The more we smother them in bubble wrap, the more physically and emotionally fragile they will become.

---

9   A lack of self-control and a high self-esteem correlate highly with personal failure, while well-disciplined willpower and dependable self-control is the single most predictable indicator of long-term success (even more than good grades, IQ or anything else). Roy T. Baumeister and John Tierny, *Willpower: Rediscovering The Greatest Human Strength* (New York: Penguin Group, 2011), 187-213.

10   **Nurture:** Our attempts to make them well-rounded has kids in an inordinate number of activities. This is expensive and offers little real return later in life. It does create anxiety and makes family togetherness almost impossible. **Competition:** This can manifest itself in overly driven parenting and often leads to parent shortcuts like helping children with their homework and school projects. **Protection:** The fear that trauma could derail a child can lead to very protective actions that stunt child development. Out of unbiblical fear of risk (both real and imagined) of injury, bad decisions, molestation, oppressive authorities or abusive peer experiences, parents can deprive children of the most important opportunities to grow in contexts with inherent risk and likely pain. Children, especially boys, need some parental protection in order to become courageous and strong adults, but much less than modern parents are comfortable with. Parents should function as advisors as much as possible rather than protectors.

If our greatest goal for our children is godly character, then we cannot allow character to be the unintended casualty of a wrongheaded parenting culture of anxiety and outright fear that assumes discipline damages kids.

The greater spiritual question is *what are we raising our children to become*? Service, hospitality and love of others are not things that the Christian Gospel teaches us to add to our lives if we've got everything else under control. Service has to be taught. Family has to be taught. We spend enormous amounts of time and money training our kids to be dancers and gymnasts and swimmers and pianists and violinists—but not servants. They are too busy for that, and so are we.

All of these good opportunities in athletics and fine arts compete with service, church, resting, deeper friendship and the family in the limited day. They are wonderful things, but just not worth it. Many of us will have to think seriously about where to pull back on some of these, or we will produce anxious children with marginal skills who will be part of weak families. If we teach our children to be great workers and athletes, that's exactly what they will be.

> We spend enormous amounts of time and money training our kids to be dancers and gymnasts and swimmers and pianists and violinists—but not servants.

A FINAL ENCOURAGEMENT

I know that last bit might have hurt. I'm struggling with that one every day. But I want to end with an encouragement: everything you do in the proper roles of your life are forms of service, not just the things you do through the organization of the church. Doing a job that contributes to the well-being of others is a worthwhile service whether it is in commerce, government or sanitation. There are a few jobs that are parasitic, and Christians should avoid them. But the majority of jobs are ways in which we make the lives of others better. We can take comfort in that and work as though that was our main priority, rather than our wage.

This is also true of all your other roles. Being a good spouse, being a wise parent, a dependable friend or a morally upright person are right and proper actions that are worthwhile service in and of themselves. Many of the most important acts of service that you will do in your life will be normal repetitions. You will do them 10,000 times. But if they are your right duties in the role God has given, they are your acceptable service to God.

Don't let your duties keep you from serving the city and the poor. Don't let discouragement deter you from editing your leisure, rethinking your parenting and including people in the daily life of your home. There is a happiness and contentment to be found in doing our real duties in our right roles out of love for God shown to our neighbor.

QUESTIONS TO THINK ABOUT

1. What does sacrificial living look like in the most practical way?

2. What are we practically raising our kids to become?

    For example, though she came from a great family, my wife was inculcated with the disciplines of being a good worker but almost none of the disciplines of the home life. Similarly, some men have little notion of leading a hospitable or serving family. Whether these results are the product of default traditionalism or a feminist overreaction, neither has a sufficiently biblical notion of self-sacrifice or the prominence of the family and need to be re-examined.

3. If neither we nor our kids have time to serve anyone, what do we do?

4. What are some practical ways we can apply the Gospel to the time we focus on leisure?

5. Can you think of any opportunities for living out the Gospel that you've missed for the sake of guarding your privacy or time alone? What's one opportunity you can pursue this week, or one behavior you can change to make room for more opportunities?

DAY 5

Service and the Understanding Progression

Jesus answered, "My teaching is not my own. It comes from him who sent me. If anyone chooses to do God's will, he will find out whether my teaching comes from God or whether I speak on my own."

John 7:16-17

OUR DESIRE FOR EXPLANATIONS

Which comes first, understanding or obedience? Don't you wish it was that easy? We normally think of understanding coming before obedience. It's one of our first negotiation instincts. My kids always want an explanation before they obey. They're usually disappointed. They need to learn to obey their parents without an explanation, and in most cases, it's much easier to explain why after they have obeyed, if any explanation is still needed.

Jesus seems to think that this is not merely a parent-child dynamic, but the way much of life's deeper learning takes place. Many wise and true things we are commanded to do don't *sound* wise or true when we hear them. Sometimes there is no way to know before you try. This is one reason why faith is often more important than information in practical learning.

OUR NEED OF EXPERIENCE

Information is only as useful as our ability to interpret it, pick out the most critical points and put it together. In the absence of experience, we are often dependent on an experienced teacher. In order to make progress, the first step is trusting the teacher.[1]

---

1 This is seen in educational institutions. In some departments, pure academics are the norm, but in other departments, experience is key. We want business professors who started companies. We want anthropology professors who lived in the jungle. We want law professors who clerked for a Supreme Court justice.

However, even when we trust the teacher, we often need to obey before we can really understand. A certain realization comes with the experience of *doing* the teaching that causes us to really understand it. Sometimes, even then we don't really understand *why* it works, we just experience that it *does* work or is true.

For example, an anesthetist friend told me we still aren't sure why anesthesia works. Apparently there are five theories on why it works, none of which can yet be proven. You can only work in that field if you're willing to learn by authority and experience.

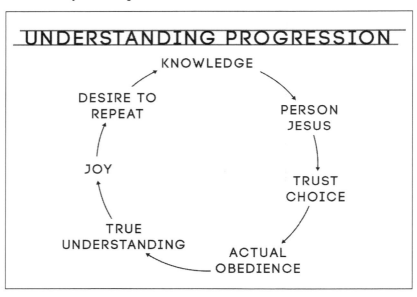

THE UNDERSTANDING PROGRESSION

This means the progression of understanding is not:

Information → Knowledge → Understanding → Belief+Trust in Teacher

Jesus says, "If anyone chooses to do God's will, [then] he will find out whether my teaching comes from God or whether I speak on my own" (John 7:17).

That is, "You will find out whether my teaching is true *when you do it.*" Obedience precedes understanding.

This is the plain and pressing reason why sacrificial service is so important in the Christian life. You can't really understand the Gospel and what you learn in the Bible *until you do it.* When we put it into practice and experience the results, then our understanding deepens and our heart and mind begin to agree with what Jesus teaches.

HOW WE BECOME WISE

This means that information still comes first on the Understanding Progression. You have to know something before you can consider what to do with it. But we rarely accept new knowledge as a result of fully understanding it. We normally accept new knowledge on the authority from which it comes. Some people bristle at this notion—that we mainly believe authorities—but it is true of virtually everything we know. There is just no way for humans to derive or verify all of the information we gather every day. We can't, and we don't. Therefore, the quality of your knowledge is enormously dependent on the wisdom of whom or what you trust.

So we can't wait to obey everything Jesus says until we prove it or really "get it." If we obey only after we approve of something, we are proving Jesus isn't the master; our understanding is. There is a big difference between listening to Jesus as a personal consultant and trusting him as a wise and loving father.

The very real problem with this way of learning is that it cannot be used by someone who wants to learn only through normal human explanation or personally directed experimentation. Jesus is saying his ways can only be understood through a combination of authoritative teaching and obedient experimentation with the direction of the Holy Spirit. It can only be proven when it's tried. To try it requires obeying some direction or command of Jesus that you don't really understand or particularly like.

> Obedience precedes understanding.

OBEDIENCE IS RISKING THROUGH TRUST

The next step is just to do it. Make a choice to trust Jesus and actually obey him. Then observe what's happening while you obey, but be patient and wait for the thing to work out. You will usually find that some unexpected dynamic made it work out differently than you expected, and you can see how God might use it to teach you and to help you understand his ways. When this happens, you not only gain the benefit, but there is a joy that comes from feeling like you just received something from God; you just received a gift of wisdom you will never lose. That joy leads to repeating the cycle, and the process goes on and on.

So the question is, where have you been holding off obeying Jesus because you don't think you agree with him? Which of these have to do with serving others? Are you ready to trust and obey him so that you can understand these commands? Which one are you going to start with? And last, when are you going to do it?

WEEK 6
SERVE
REACH THE WORLD

Following Jesus doesn't just compel us to connect, grow and serve. Jesus calls us to help others do the same. We are here to help people connect with God and others. We are here to help others grow in their understanding of the Gospel and knowledge of the Bible, and to help them serve the city and reach the world. Jesus uses what he does *to us* to do the same things *through us* in concert with the local church. We are here to reach the world *together*.

WEEK 6
SERVE
REACH THE WORLD

SERMON NOTES

WEEK 6
SERVE
REACH THE WORLD
SMALL GROUP
DISCUSSION QUESTIONS

WATCH THE SMALL GROUP VIDEO

1. In the Day 3 reading it says there are two great obstacles that keep us from embracing global missions. Either we are made to feel or are told that we don't have the right to do global missions or we feel like the task is insurmountable. Which have you experienced or which are you more prone to feel? Why?

2. The video discusses four convictions we need to have about global missions. Which do you think or not think about? Do any intimidate you? How can we incorporate these if we haven't already into our church, small group or individual lives?
   i. We have a global mandate.
   ii. We have the right to fulfill the global mandate.
   iii. We have the ability from God to accomplish the global mandate.
   iv. We have the privilege, that we share with Jesus, of doing the global mandate.

3. The video also discusses eight ways to live out the four convictions together in the local church. Which do you think is most important for you to live out right now?

    i. Be part of a church that knows it's part of something bigger.

    ii. Embrace the "support a missionary" purpose of small groups.

    iii. Engage in dependent prayer. We need to ask God for his power because we know we need him.

    iv. Stop being ashamed of the Gospel.

    v. Quit being ashamed of missions and missionaries.

    vi. Sacrifically serve others for missional reasons.

    vii. Become less fragile and consumeristic Christians so we don't consume unnecessary resources that could be used to do the mission.

    viii. Participate in sacrificial giving.

4. A goal for us as a church is to have 15% of our budget dedicated to global missions in the next five years. There are three ways we can accomplish this. How can you incorporate at least one of these into your life individually and into your small group?

    i. We need to make global missions a high priority.

    ii. We need to do ministry ourselves so that we spend less money on ourselves.

    iii. We need to engage in a deep and disciplined generosity.

DAY 1
The Heart of the Matter

> But the LORD said, "You have been concerned about this vine, though you did not tend it or make it grow. It sprang up overnight and died overnight. But Nineveh has more than a hundred and twenty thousand people who cannot tell their right hand from their left, and many cattle as well. Should I not be concerned about that great city?"
>
> Jonah 4:10-11

FRAMING THE HEART OF THE MATTER

For years, I thought I knew what the book of Jonah was about. A man is told to go to a certain place, and he instead tries to run from God. God sends a storm and an enormous fish and forcefully puts Jonah back on course. The moral of this story? Go where God sends you, or you're fish food! God redirects disobedience with discomfort. That's what I thought, at least. But while that is a part of the story, it's not the *heart* of this book, and it is not the main thing God wants us to learn from the story of this ancient man and an evil city.

We need a little background. Jonah was sent to a city called Nineveh (modern day Mosul, Iraq), which was one of the two main imperial cities of the Assyrian empire, the dominant nation in the world at that time. The Assyrians came to power through the use of some of the most revolting kinds of warfare imaginable and are sometimes referred to as literally the most brutal nation in human history. Even the Nazis have to bow in inferiority to Assyrian brutality. Their treatment of cities that did not surrender immediately to their armies and pay heavy tributes to the kingdom made rape and murder seem civilized.[1]

To add to this, Jonah was a patriotic prophet. He is mentioned along with this description of Jeroboam II, one of Israel's kings:

> *He did evil in the eyes of the Lord...He was the one who restored the boundaries of Israel...in accordance with the word of the LORD...spoken through his servant Jonah...*
>
> 2 Kings 14:24-25

These short verses make two things evident. First, Jonah became known within Israel as a patriotic prophet of national victory and prosperity. Second, we see that Israel continued to decline in faith and morality. Israel was doing well materially and militarily, but it continued careening toward God's judgment.

As the Assyrian empire grew, it was inevitable that its armies would soon reach Israel. Israel was pushing back their smaller neighbors, but the dark clouds of the Assyrian storm were moving. So, when God's word came to Jonah, he immediately knew the significance of this assignment. He knew that if he preached against the city of Nineveh, and they repented, then Assyria would not only escape judgment for the atrocities they had already committed, but they could potentially go on to devour his home.

What would you have done? Honestly.

THE REAL REASON

You see, we often read this book too piously, and we don't see what an awful job God had given Jonah to do.[2]

---

1   In ancient warfare, sieges were terribly costly for the attacking force. Cities that surrendered without being breached, therefore, were treated with leniency, while cities that had to be breached were usually massacred. The Assyrians did even worse so their reputation would make conquest easier. Assyrian battle art depicts piles of human hands, eyes being gouged out, pregnant women being cut open, impaling of humans in many ways (including through their bowels, which slowly killed victims over several days). We should keep this in mind while we try to identify with Jonah in how much he hated them.

2   Though it is no more awful or difficult than the job he gave himself in the person of the Son.

Jonah ran because he couldn't ignore the message, but he couldn't bear to deliver it. He could not imagine being part of redeeming such a horrible people.

And here is the crushing theme of the book: the real reason we reject God's will is that we care more about our own interests. If we take time to examine our lives carefully, we will find that we are more like this ancient prophet than we care to imagine. We think God should be partial to us. We are his really special people. If it isn't good for us, it can't be his will.

Essentially, Jonah rejected the task God gave him because that task was not good for Jonah, his family, or his country, and I think this is the same reason we often don't reach out to our city. Sacrificially reaching the city will personally cost us or expose us to some kind of risk. Reaching poor kids means they will be around our kids. If we include homeless people, they will be hanging around. If we form a ministry for hurting or addicted people, we will have high maintenance people with baggage wanting our friendship. If we do service projects, something else in our overbooked lives will inevitably have to go.

This is the argument Jonah has with God, except the stakes are much higher. For Jonah, the stakes are the well-being of his family and nation versus the lives of 120,000 people who are ignorant of God's truth. God forces Jonah to go to Assyria and preach condemnation on the city, and to his disgust the people of Nineveh respond and repent. They humble themselves greatly and cry out to the Lord for mercy. Jonah knows that this means their nation will survive for at least another generation.

We think we are virtuous and noble, but our priorities are actually completely rooted in self-interest and self-preservation.

Jonah may be the only prophet in the Old Testament who was successful in leading his audience to repentance and didn't want to be. He stands as a memorable example of humanity's universal and terrible attitude problem. We think we are virtuous and noble, but our priorities are actually completely rooted in self-interest and self-preservation. Getting in-touch with our real motivations can be a humiliating and sobering experience.

ON LOVING SHADE MORE THAN GOD

Seeing the Assyrians repent and avoid the destruction they deserved was more than Jonah could take. When he saw that the city would not be destroyed, he threw a fit. At this point, Jonah might come off as a baby to you, but don't blow him off. The man's legacy has been destroyed, he's been in a fish's stomach, he's traveled more than 600 miles to a foreign nation he hates, and now his worst nightmare is coming true: They are listening to him. Jonah isn't just being a baby. He snaps.

Then God asks him a very calm and humbling question, "Have you any right to be angry?" (Jonah 4:4). Jonah doesn't answer, so God uses a vine to make his point. It grows up and gives him shade from the very hot sun. Jonah is pleased with the vine. The next day, God withers the vine. Jonah gets dehydrated, overheated and angry.

God asks him another question, "Do you have a right to be angry about the vine?" Instead of defending his *right* to be angry, he ignores the question and restates the *amount* of anger he feels: "I am angry enough to die" (Jonah 4:9).

God replies, "You have been concerned about this vine, though you did not tend it or make it grow. It sprang up overnight and died overnight" (4:10). Essentially, God asks about Jonah's connection to the vine. What connected you to it that makes your anger just? Did you make it? Cause it to grow? Was it intrinsically valuable? Jonah only valued it for what it did for him. It was useful for his comfort, so when it was taken away, he was mad. God is confronting this man about the defective heart he is carrying around.

There he was, halfway around the world, suffering in the heat, alone on a hillside, realizing that he loved a plant more than he loved God. Jonah had to face the realization that he literally cared more about his shade than he cared about the lives of 120,000 morally ignorant and lost people who mattered to God. To Jonah these Assyrians were nothing but a threat, but God knew them as needy and had compassion on them, making no apology for caring about these people.

SEEING YOURSELF IN JONAH

That's where the book ends: "Should I not be concerned about that great city?" (Jonah 4:11). If Jonah responded, it's not recorded. We are just left with this man lying on the side of a hill, dying of heat, watching a wicked people get mercy while he is being rebuked by God. It is a sad ending, and it is supposed to be. It's supposed to make us think about our own hearts. We are supposed to be embarrassed by God's final words and realize that our compassion for the lost is too mixed up in our own interests. Our love for our city is motivated by our love for ourselves, our children and our sub-culture rather than by love for God.

It's a great irony that God sends Jonah to call a city to repentance, and the book ends with Jonah's own call to repentance. Isn't it just as possible that God would say something similar to us about our concerns?

The book has an ironic and depressing ending, but that doesn't mean Jonah's story ended there. Jonah is a historical book. Have you ever considered who wrote it? Only one person could have written this book: Jonah. How could he have written such a humiliating book about himself unless he finally came to understand and love the God who humbled him on that hillside in ancient Iraq?

I think one way to see all of Jonah's hatred for God is to think that when he later wrote his story, it was out of an equal depth of love. I think we can see that he came to love the God about whom he had once complained and wrote with great irony, "I knew that you are a gracious and compassionate God, slow to anger and abounding in love, a God who relents from sending calamity" (Jonah 4:2). What was once a scoff became a song.

DAY 2

Dependent Prayer:
Praying For The City and The World

Seek the peace and prosperity of the city to which I have carried you into exile. Pray to the LORD for it, because if it prospers, you too will prosper.

Jeremiah 29:7

READ JEREMIAH 29:7, MATTHEW 5:43-45, LUKE 6:27-36, 1 TIMOTHY 2:1-4

The Bible has a lot to say about one particular piece of seeking the prosperity of our city. It's clear that praying for our civic and political leaders is foundational in this goal. Why is it important? The above passages give three reasons.

First, in Jeremiah 29, we are told to pray for the city because our fate is bound to its fate. We've covered this some in previous weeks. In this life, our welfare is not only determined individually but is tied to the community that we live in. Christianity teaches the fundamental connectedness of all people. Though the redeemed and the rebellious will inevitably be separated in the future, they are inoperably linked now (Matthew 13:24-30). We have to see even our enemies as our God-chosen neighbors and pray for their good, peace and prosperity, hoping that kindness will lead them toward repentance (Romans 2:4).

The second reason we should pray even for our enemies and persecutors is that by doing so we will be "sons of [our] Father in heaven" (Matthew 5:45). In the ancient world, a son did what his father did. To know if a man would be a good husband for your daughter, you didn't look at him, you looked at his father. There was no public school, so boys grew up with their fathers. They learned their father's trade and his character, and so came the saying, "like father, like son." This is the major connotation of "sonship" in the Bible.

So Jesus is saying that when we pray for our enemies, we imitate God's character and trade. We show we are becoming loving toward people undeserving of love (like he already is), and we are embracing the spiritual and moral trade of redemption (like he does). We are becoming his sons and daughters, the most dignified things we could be. We are becoming like Jesus, the perfect son.

The third reason to pray for the city is for our relationship with our culture. In 1 Timothy 2, Paul tells us that we should pray for and love our leaders so that they will allow us to live godly lives. At different times in the Christian story, civil authorities have interfered (and will continue to interfere) with the practical application of Christian spirituality and morality, and we should pray that this won't happen so that we will not have to be in conflict with our government and civil society.[1]

Then, in 1 Timothy 2:3-4, the apostle links our peace with the salvation of the people of the city, especially its leaders. If our prayers come to pass, then the lack of conflict between us and our cultural neighbors will create a greater opportunity for their salvation. Whenever possible, we should openly thank God for them and act as a priest for them, bringing their requests to God.

I have a friend named John. He lives in Mumbai, India, where being Christian is technically legal, but practicing it sometimes is not. For example, telling people about Jesus is against the law. Even if you are in the children's home you built, talking with little girls you saved from the red light district who were dying of tuberculosis, it's against the law if their parents were Hindus.

John has tried to put these verses into practice in some very touchy situations. First, he has linked his fortune to the fortune of the city. The main ministry he offers is a

---

1   This is both to prevent our suffering persecution and also to prevent them from becoming guilty of punishing Christians for living godly lives.

children's home. He takes in not just Christian children, but all needy children. Parents, police, politicians and even gangsters have put children in his care, and he takes them all. He knows that his life and prosperity are bound to the city where God has planted him.

But John's work invites persecution. A while back, he was trying to build a boys' home. He hired a metal worker who was working at a good price, but was not the guy approved by the local political gangster. A lower party boss threatened both John's life and the worker's, so John prayed for everyone involved. Later on, the same party boss dragged back the terrified worker and told him, "You must do this work and finish it now." Both were bewildered.

It turns out that word got back to the main party boss. This man called in the underling and read him the riot act. His reason was simply, "Don't you know that the Christian's god is a very powerful god? Right now these people and the children *pray for us*. If you threaten them, they may call out to their god *against us*! Go back and win their favor, because I will not make an enemy of the Christian god."

Now, that is a very normal Hindu way of thinking. But the event was a perfect example of the application of these principles in a much more difficult situation than most of us will face.

DEPENDENT PRAYER

This is one of my favorite quotes on prayer:

> [T]he minimal prayer accompanying many projects in the church may indicate that what is being undertaken is simply what human beings can accomplish pretty well by themselves... [T]hose who do the work seem fully confident that they can produce good results simply by their talent, expertise and effort.[2]

If our plans don't force us to pray, then we probably don't think we need God to get them done. We need bigger plans

---

2 Lovelace, *Dynamics of Spiritual Life*, 153.

or different plans, or we need to wake up to the fact that we are not going to be able to accomplish anything without his empowerment. The Bible tells us in fairly explicit terms that none of the results we seek can be accomplished without God's power and activity. On numerous occasions in the Bible, God demonstrates that before we receive his help, he often requires us to ask for it explicitly.

We may pray, but do we pray *dependently*? Is there anything in our life that we really believe *requires* God's activity, for which our skills and ability are wholly insufficient? There is no command in the Bible for how long one must pray. I believe it's legalism to charge that someone should pray a certain number of minutes or hours a day, but I also believe it's idolatry for us to go through a whole day and for it not to occur to us to pray. It should alert us to too high a view of ourselves and our abilities and too low a view of God's activity and our need for his help. Or it may reveal that we are not consciously participating in God's seemingly impossible purposes in love, mercy and mission, because those things will always make us long for someone with bigger arms to do the heavy lifting.

> God will always call us to things for which we will need him.

Jesus once said that his burden is light, yet for so many it feels heavy. I think that might be because God intended for us to do the lighter lifting of prayer so that he would do the heavy lifting in things that would otherwise be impossible. Neglect of prayer is designed to break our backs, not so that we will turn away from God, but so that we will turn to him. God will always call us to things for which we will need him. This is why bold action must always be accompanied by bold prayer.

FOR FURTHER REFLECTION

1. Do you pray for your city, leaders and world?

2. What in your life *drives* you to pray?

3. Why that thing and not other things?

4. How can you change your thinking, feeling or practice so that asking God for help and leadership is your *first* impulse?

DAY 3

To The Islands:
The Gospel Without Borders

*May God be gracious to us and bless us and make his
face shine upon us, that your ways may be known
on earth, your salvation among all nations. May the
peoples praise you, O God; may all the peoples praise
you. May the nations be glad and sing for joy, for you
rule the peoples justly and guide the nations of the
earth.*

Psalm 67:1-4

*Here is my servant, whom I uphold, my chosen one
in whom I delight; I will put my Spirit on him and he
will bring justice to the nations. He will not shout or
cry out, or raise his voice in the streets. A bruised reed
he will not break, and a smoldering wick he will not
snuff out. In faithfulness he will bring forth justice;
he will not falter or be discouraged till he establishes
justice on earth. In his law the islands will put their
hope.*

Isaiah 42:1-4

*Jesus came to them and said, "All authority in heaven
and on earth has been given to me. Therefore go and
make disciples of all nations."*

Matthew 28:18-19

A MESSAGE WITHOUT BORDERS

The message of Jesus is a message without borders.
The prayer in Psalm 67 is that God would bless us and be
gracious to us, and this request has a clear purpose. Notice the "that" which starts the second verse. The reason the
writer wants God to be gracious to us and to bless us is so
that God's ways would be known on earth among all the

nations.[1] He doesn't consider it cultural aggression or imperialism because he believes God already rules over all the nations. His great hope is that if God is gracious to us and blesses us, the nations will realize this fact, trust in God and eternally enjoy him. This desire is both right and compassionate, because God is not only their rightful ruler., he is a good and just ruler.

From the beginning to the end of the Bible, all of humanity is in view. The Bible doesn't begin with Abraham, the first Jew. It begins with Adam and Eve, the first humans and the parents of all nations. The visions in Revelation end not in the final redemption of the Jews alone, but in worship of the one to whom they sang,

> *You are worthy to take the scroll and to open its seals, because you were slain, and with your blood you purchased men for God from every tribe and language and people and nation. You have made them to be a kingdom and priests[2] to serve our God, and they will reign on the earth.*
>
> Revelation 5:9-10

The story starts with the creation of the first humans and ends with the redemption of people from all of humanity into a single nation belonging to God.

In the book of Isaiah, God refers to his relationship with "the islands" in fourteen different verses. Isaiah 49, the passage about Jesus the Savior, starts out not with a call for just the Jewish people to listen, but with this call: "Listen to me, you islands; hear this, you distant nations..." The message is for the furthest possible people groups. It is for the most

---

1   "Nations" in the Bible does not usually refer to empires or nation states. It refers to what anthropologists call "ethno linguistic groups," that is, groups that are of similar ethnicity, distinct culture and speak the same language. A group would be a different "nation" if cultural, linguistic or ethnic barriers needed to be crossed to reach them. Christian ministers who have been trained to do this work are usually called "missionaries."

2   This is a reference to the promise (Exodus 19:6) that through Abraham there would be a nation of priests. This ties the whole plan of redemption together from the first "man of faith," Abraham, to the final gathering of all those with faith in the promise of redemption that came from Abraham's God. See also Revelation 1:6.

forgotten people on the most distant and tiny islands. It is for everyone.

THE DELIVERY

Perhaps even more shocking is not the "what" but the "how." Jesus claimed that he would accomplish this through his Church, his disciples—us. He shares his vision of the Church in Acts 1:8: "But you will receive power when the Holy Spirit comes on you; and *you will be my witnesses* in Jerusalem, and in all Judea and Samaria, and to the ends of the earth." Jesus says that he will build his Church, a group of people called out of the world as a special people of God, and "the gates of Hades [hell] will not overcome it" (Matthew 16:18). The work of Gospel expansion belongs to Jesus, but he chooses to do it through the people of his Church.

This is precisely the content of the commission Jesus gave his disciples before he ascended after his resurrection:

> And this gospel of the kingdom will be preached **in the whole world as a testimony to all nations**, and then the end will come. ... Then Jesus came to them and said, "All authority in heaven and on earth has been given to me. Therefore go and make disciples of all nations, baptizing them in the name of the Father and of the Son and of the Holy Spirit, and teaching them to obey everything I have commanded you. And surely I am with you always, to the very end of the age."
>
> Matthew 28:14, 18-20

THE TWO OBSTACLES

Whether we can put them into words, almost everyone either thinks or feels the same two obstacles to this charge. First, we are either made to feel or are explicitly told that we don't have the authority to do this. We'll deal with this in tomorrow's reading.

Second, the task seems insurmountable. Many feel like God isn't really with us or that the tools he has given us to use are not sufficient for the size of the task. Most Christians *feel* this more than they think it or say it. The first thing we need to see here is that this isn't a problem with our view on missions. It's a problem with our understanding of the Gospel itself.

Two of the immediate promises of the Gospel are the presence of God and authority in spiritual conflict—real spiritual power.[3] Jesus said he would never leave us nor forsake us and that the Holy Spirit would make his home within us. The Great Commission ends with, "and surely I am with you to the very end of the age." Do you notice how specific that is? He says "surely" to emphasize the trustworthiness of what he's saying. He says "I am with you" to acknowledge both the question we would be asking and the answer he is giving. And then he says "to the very end of the age" so that we will never imagine that we have outlived the duration of his promise. We will be able to tell when that promise stops because Christ will have returned.

He has left us with sufficient tools, though the tools he's given us are humble. They are designed so that only he can do the heavy lifting. We are merely to be witnesses. In one of the darker times of Paul's ministries recorded in the book of Acts, he's in the city of Corinth, and he's having a pretty difficult time. Some people have believed but there is a lot of resistance, and Paul must have been wondering if he should stay or leave.

> The tools he's given us are humble. They are designed so that only he can do the heavy lifting. We are merely to be witnesses.

As he sits in prison one night, God speaks to him in a vision:

> *Do not be afraid; keep on speaking, do not be silent. For I am with you, and no one is going to attack and harm you, because I have many people in this city.*
>
> Acts 18:9-10

---

3   Lovelace, *Dynamics*, 119.

Jesus wasn't referring to the people who are already Christians; there were almost none. But Jesus knew exactly what he was doing. He just needed Paul to keep doing his job, telling people the truth about Jesus as persuasively and plainly as possible. Jesus knew that many people were going to come to him, but the first thing he reminded Paul of was, "I am with you."

This promise gave Paul a very serious sense of boldness about the Gospel. He said:

> I am not ashamed of the gospel, because it is the power of God for the salvation of everyone who believes: first for the Jew, then for the Gentile.

Romans 1:16

> That is why I am suffering as I am. Yet I am not ashamed, because I know whom I have believed, and am convinced that he is able to guard what I have entrusted to him for that day.

2 Timothy 1:12

The mission still lies before every generation. The commission still carries the same authority and is supported by the same promise. The particular calling of being a cross-cultural international missionary does not fall to everyone.[4] But we are all called to the same mission. It is a mission without borders, and we need everyone.

---

4   Though we should keep in mind that it takes twenty to fifty generous givers to send one.

DAY 4

Do We Have The Right?
Are Missions and Evangelism Forces For Good?

He says: "It is too small a thing for you to be my servant to restore the tribes of Jacob and bring back those of Israel I have kept. I will also make you a light for the Gentiles, that you may bring my salvation to the ends of the earth."

Isaiah 49:6

Then Jesus came to them and said, "All authority in heaven and on earth has been given to me. Therefore go and make disciples of all nations, baptizing them in the name of the Father and of the Son and of the Holy Spirit, and teaching them to obey everything I have commanded you. And surely I am with you always, to the very end of the age."

Matthew 28:18-20

DO WE HAVE THE RIGHT?

The risen Christ has given his followers an absolute global missionary call, yet we live in a country and a moment in which many count this as a terrible public sin against humanity. Missions is often derided as a form of colonialism that damages cultures and disrespects the humanity of the people in the receiving culture. If we're interested in sharing the message of Jesus either locally (evangelism) or globally (missions), we will face strenuous objections. We are either explicitly told or made to feel that we don't have the spiritual or moral authority to do this. (I have briefly dealt with the four major objections in Appendix 5.)

We need to listen to our critics, but we need to listen to them critically without being manipulated or intimidated. Some of their objections point to things that deserve our attention. All cross-cultural initiatives (including Christian missions, military intervention, economic development, commerce, etc.) can be disruptive and damaging, some more than others. Many people claim that Christian missions mainly comprise the damaging variety of human intervention.

> We need to listen to our critics, but we need to listen to them critically without being manipulated or intimidated.

And yet, the story of *real* Western missionaries is very different. Throughout history, missionaries have been among the greatest forces for global good. John Paton was nearly killed numerous times and stood up more than once for the natives of the New Hebrides against Western traders. The native people he advocated for were cannibals who "ate a couple of their women whenever they became disobedient." He repeatedly risked his life disrupting the evils of the native culture while trying to advocate against the genocidal agendas of some of the Western merchants. In the 19th century, John McKenzie helped Khama III and two other chiefs from modern day Botswana travel to Britain to gain land protection for the native peoples against the European imperialists.

Another very stark case occurred amid the atrocities of the French and Belgian Congos. In both regions, native villages were forced to get rubber from the jungles, and the abuse of the natives was horrifically cruel. While the fact that this was happening in the French Congo went completely unnoticed by Europe, the abuse in the Belgian Congo "aroused the largest international protest movement since the abolition of slavery."[1] The difference? Protestant missionaries were only allowed in the Belgian Congo. These missionaries got the story out to people in the missions societies of their home countries.

This kind of missionary reform was so normal that the

---

1   Andrea Palpant Dilley, "The Surprising Discovery About Those Colonialist, Proselytizing Missionaries," Christianity Today, http://www.christianitytoday.com/ct/2014/january-february/world-missionaries-made.html?paging=off (accessed 15 Jul. 2014).

East India Company began to ban missionaries from all their territories because missionaries could be counted on to create moral troubles for them in their home nations. In fact, from the 1st century through the 20th century, it was often the moral disruptions Christians created in cultures that caused people to flock to faith in Christ. The moral vision of the Gospel is not a bug; it's a fixed feature. As long as people are not coerced to accept it, they should be free to hear it. Jesus was clear: Our job is to witness. Conversion is their choice.

ON WHOSE AUTHORITY?

But it's not the track record of historical missionaries that give us the authority to bring the message of the Gospel to the farthest islands. In Isaiah 49:6, God says to the Messiah servant, "It is too small a thing for you to be my servant to restore the tribes of Jacob...I will also make you a *light for the Gentiles,*[2] that you may bring my salvation *to the ends of the earth.*" Hundreds of years before Jesus was born, God said the Messiah would have authority to bring God's salvation to the very ends of the earth. Jesus tells us that we will be the lights who will carry the message of what he has done "to the ends of the earth" (Acts 1:8). We have the authority to do it because Jesus has the authority to give us that authority.

Notice what Jesus said to start Matthew 28:18, quoted above. He starts out the commission by explicitly defeating one of the first objections people would make against his witnesses: "Who gave you authority to do this?" Matthew reminds us that they questioned Jesus' authority (Matthew 21:23), and they will question ours. That's why Jesus started out his commission by saying, "All authority in heaven and on earth has been given to me. Therefore..." (Matthew 28:18). Jesus has all authority everywhere, and in that authority, he commands us to go and make disciples of all nations. Therefore, no one has the authority to tell us we can't

---

2   "Gentiles" simply refers to all the nations or people groups of the entire world that are not Jewish. The Hebrew word *goyim* literally means a "people" or a "nation." It corresponds to the generic Greek word *ethnos,* which also is a generic referent to "nations."

do this.

No one can override Jesus. No matter how politically powerful, academically influential or religiously cynical the attack, it need have no effect on us. We can say what the apostles said when their authority was questioned by the government authorities: "Judge for yourselves whether it is right in God's sight to obey you rather than God" (Acts 4:19). Our authority to fulfill the local and global mandate comes from a higher authority than any person, philosophy or government. It comes from someone who has all the authority in both heaven and on earth.

A CONSCIOUS AND INTENTIONALLY MISSIONAL PEOPLE

One danger in the missionary call is that some lesser authority will intimidate us or persuade us to give it up. An even more common danger is that we will become unintentional and passive. Both sharing the Gospel and being interested in people we have never met require intentional and disciplined character lived out in line with biblical values. Evangelism and missions have to be intentional parts of our community life as a church. If they aren't, we will close our mouths and forget the world. That is the gravitational pull of our human nature.

Jesus gave his authority to us because he wanted us to use it, and he wanted us to use it in keeping with his character and purposes. It is tempting to feel like this is a burden. If it is, it is one in which we suffer with Christ. His real intention was to make the authority he gave us so clear that it would set us free. He wanted you and me to be free and unconflicted in living out his global commission, no matter what the opposition and no matter what comforts may call us away from it. As always, God seems to be more interested in supplying courage than ease. It is exactly what a conscious and intentionally missional people require.

DAY 5

Gospel Passions and the Healthy Church

"A person preaches well only that word which he preaches well to his own soul. And he that does not feed on and thrive in the digestion of the spiritual food which he provides for others will not be able to make their mouths water for the meal he serves. In fact, he does not even know if the food he provides is poisonous, unless he has really tasted of it himself. If the word does not dwell with power in us, it will not pass with power from us."

John Owen[1]

Or, a modern summary:

"Never trust a skinny cook."

Unknown

"If we get better, people will demand our influence grow."

Truett Cathy

*"We have to get **better** before we get **bigger**."*

Andy Stanley[2]

One of my first jobs in college was as a camp counselor in the Adirondack Mountains. The head cook was Margaret Gingrich. Margaret had a funny thing she said whenever anybody complimented something she cooked. Somebody

---

1   John Owen, *The Works of John Owen*, ed. William H. Goold, (Edinburgh: Banner of Truth, 1965), XVI: 76. Original language: "A man preacheth that sermon only well unto others which preacheth itself in his own soul. And he that doth not feed on and thrive in the digestion of the food which he provides for others will scarce make it savoury unto them; yea, he knows not but the food he hath provided may be poison, unless he have really tasted of it himself. If the word do not dwell with power in us, it will not pass with power from us."

2   Andy Stanley, *Better Before Bigger*, podcast audio, May, 3, 2013, http://andystanley.com/free-resources/

would say, "Margaret, this is great!" and she would never reply, "Thank you," or "I'm glad you like it." She would always say, in an excited tone, "Isn't it?!"

That reply told us two things: First, *she was humble.* The food was more important than the cook because her first impulse was to celebrate the food, not her achievement. Second, *she had been eating it herself.* She had nourished herself on it, and she knew exactly how good it was. I can still hear her saying it while wearing that apron emblazoned with "Never trust a skinny cook." Never indeed, whether for natural food or spiritual.

People will rarely be healthier or stronger than the wholesomeness and nourishment available in what they eat. Whether we are bringing something to our neighbors or to the nations, *we had better focus as much on the quality of the export as we do on the action of exporting it.* We're not doing anyone any favors when we pass on our poisons, defects and pathologies. The Bible uses metaphors like feeding and reproduction to describe the ways people come to and grow in faith.[3] We naturally come to look like the people who lead us, and we want the people we're leading in faith to be whole and healthy. If missions, global and local,[4] is a kind of spiritual reproduction, we can't help but produce something like ourselves.

In that sense, the best "missions churches" will simply be deeply healthy churches, because a church that is centered on the Gospel has the Gospel fueling everything. Just as the Gospel motivates and builds worship, community and a

---

3   See for example: Matthew 13; Mark 4; Luke 6:43-45, 13:18-21; John 15; Corinthians 3:2, 6-8; Colossians 2:19; 1 Peter 2:2-3.

4   Bringing the Gospel message to people locally is usually referred to as "evangelism," which literally means, "to good news someone." The word "missions" is often used of global missions. The main distinction isn't distance, but culture or specialized context. We usually call something "missions" when a special action needs to be taken for the message to penetrate a new group of people because some barrier exists. In such cases a "missionary" is needed, someone who has trained not only in the Gospel message, but in the special barrier-crossing knowledge necessary to reach the receptor group. This training can include language, education, cultural knowledge and practices, customs, and so on.

desire to know and love God, it will also create and motivate our desires to serve and to reach. Whatever a church's written mission statement is, an understood commitment to a Gospel foundation can never be far away. It could read something like this: "The Gospel about the life, death and resurrection of Jesus must *form*, *prioritize* and *motivate* everything we are and do." It doesn't necessarily need to be etched on a plaque, but it had better be engraved on our minds.

> The passions that God creates in us will always either *radiate from* the Gospel, or they will *compete with* each other.

Why is this? It is because the passions that God creates in us will always either *radiate from* the Gospel, or they will *compete with* each other. God, as displayed in Christ and the Gospel, will either be our shared passion or we will fight over our subsidiary passions.

THE DELTA EFFECT

I've been a fly fisherman since I was a kid. That means wading in rivers. The funny thing about wading in rivers is that the speed doesn't matter nearly as much as the depth. You can easily wade across a ten-inch-deep stream that's really moving, but you'll never make it across a three-foot-deep stream that's barely moving. Momentum is produced by unified depth. Pressure washers move dirt. Rivers move ships.

However, the one place where rivers don't move ships is at the delta. Deltas spread rivers out, leaving them shallow and weak. A similar phenomenon happens in the Church. Churches experience the Delta Effect when they focus not on the Gospel itself, but on particular applications that the Gospel motivates. Let's consider five examples of things the Gospel motivates that churches tend to focus on:

1. **Worship and Prayer:** Direct communication to and valuing of God

2. **Evangelism and Missions:** Sharing the message with

all people

3. **Discipleship and Doctrine:** Being formed in Gospel truth and practice

4. **Mercy and Justice:** Ethical application of the Gospel to one's neighbor

5. **Cultural Renewal and Engagement:** Gospel application to one's culture

All five of these things will be operating in a healthy Gospel movement and will be real interests of a mature Christian. However, Christians will not be equally involved in all of these things simultaneously. The foundational passion of every Christian should be the glory and rule of the crucified and risen Jesus and the good news that he saves and redeems all people who will believe, and ultimately, all of the physical creation in a new heaven and a new earth. However, the secondary or subsidiary passion of Christians vary based on how that truth interacts with their experiences, temperament, education, interests and so on. This is where things tend to go awry. We tend to cluster as Christians around our subsidiary passions.

> Momentum is produced by unified depth.

When this happens, we end up with special interest silos within churches, or worse and more commonly, different churches take on the personality of one of these five applications. We get worship and prayer churches. We get serious Bible and discipleship churches. We get seeker-focused evangelistic churches, social action churches and churches focused on family, Christian education and Christian politics. All good. All impoverished by themselves. Any effect of all these different churches is blunted by the fact that they are spread out and shallow like a river delta. There is no power, little impact and insufficient motivation for great Gospel effect. However, there is plenty of self-righteousness, fighting over budgets and other phenomena that accompany disunity.

THE CHALLENGE OF UNITY IN DIVERSITY

The above emphases will either radiate out as legitimate applications of the Gospel, or they will inevitably compete with each other for the heart of the movement, destroying the movement's health, power, clarity and beauty, and detracting from God's proper glory.

Think about it: Where do you find the people to do mercy and compassion ministries? Who gathers them, and how do they come to have the deep Gospel motivation that makes them keep showing up? You need evangelism and discipleship for that. If you spend all your time worshiping and praying, are you really obeying the Gospel's mission mandate? If you're strong in evangelism, but you don't do discipleship, where do you think new believers will be in a year? When we focus exclusively on discipling people in how to study the Bible, we can lose sight of orienting the heart through worship and prayer toward the one about whom Scripture is written. That neglect tends to lead either to self-righteousness or to believing that studying the Bible is an end in itself when it should lead to worship, prayer, compassion and evangelism. And if we focus on worship, evangelism and discipleship while paying no attention to the larger effect on the family, education, politics and culture, how long will it take for us to lose touch with the public mind we are ignoring and yet evangelizing? How can we expect people to live out Christian discipleship wisely in the public sphere? All five applications of the Gospel flow out of the Gospel and feed the momentum of each other.

Still, we want people to be enormously passionate about their subsidiary passions and the applications of the Gospel to which they are most committed. Each of these applications require people deeply committed to them and ready to make sacrifices in living them out. But how do you get a healthy unified movement when people really do embrace their sub-passions and give themselves to them sacrificially? Are you always going to have fighting? Aren't people always going to sort into silos or different churches?

Ultimately, this is the fundamental problem of unity in

diversity. Our culture treats diversity like it's always a good thing. In fact, diversity is both one of the most strengthening and destructive phenomena in the world. It ceases to be destructive and becomes strengthening when the diversity is organized around a constructive unifying principle. When the Church is truly centered on the Gospel, unity in diversity is really possible. People see their subsidiary passions as flowing out from the Gospel, and they realize that this is true of the other passions represented around them. People see the conflict between them not as a battle to be won or a problem to be solved, but as a tension to be managed.

Gospel-centeredness doesn't just produce five or more applications, it also motivates, organizes and prioritizes those applications. The more we understand the Gospel, its multiple legitimate applications and how it is motivated, organized and prioritized in the Scriptures, the more it will produce the application most necessary for true unity in diversity: humility.

Only then can the church really be on mission in a way that is healthy and powerful. When Jesus and the message of salvation unifies and motivates all of our gifts and passions, the Church will flow like a powerful river of grace and truth for the healing of the nations.

> The message of Jesus is too good and too urgent to linger.

We have to go and send out. The nations can't wait. The message of Jesus is too good and too urgent to linger. But spiritually speaking, no one in their right mind should trust a spiritually skinny cook. How can they accept from us something we have not obviously nourished ourselves with? If we grow in godliness, courage, passion and humility, people will demand we come. While we seek to make the message bigger, we can never stop seeking to live the message better.

EPILOGUE
THE END OF THE BOOK

Therefore, since we are surrounded by such a great cloud of witnesses, let us throw off everything that hinders and the sin that so easily entangles, and let us run with perseverance the race marked out for us. Let us fix our eyes on Jesus, the author and perfecter of our faith, who for the joy set before him endured the cross, scorning its shame, and sat down at the right hand of the throne of God. Consider him who endured such opposition from sinful men, so that you will not grow weary and lose heart.

Hebrews 12:1-3

"Sacrificial service is the price of influence."

High Point Church axiom

The church holds the deposit of the good news: the Gospel. She is made up of the people who believe the testimony "that God was reconciling the world to himself in Christ, not counting men's sins against them," and who live in the knowledge that "he has committed to us the message of reconciliation" (2 Corinthians 5:19).

So why do so many people (including us) act like our good news isn't good? Part of the reason is because we are predisposed against it by our sin. This is the point of John 3:19-21:

This is the verdict: Light has come into the world, but men loved darkness instead of light because their deeds were evil. Everyone who does evil hates the light, and will not come into the light for fear that his

deeds will be exposed. But whoever lives by the truth
comes into the light, so that it may be seen plainly
that what he has done has been done through God.

The normal human attitude is to run from the light, and if we live by the truth, it's because of what God has done for and in us.

But another practical reason people don't act like the good news is good is that our lifestyles don't always communicate good news. We talk about the love of Christ, but we aren't loving. We claim the generous God as our King, but we aren't generous. We claim the humble God as our Master while behaving arrogantly and independently.

I don't think this is an accident. I think we should expect the religion of the truthful and humble God to be one you really can't fake. Jesus was the most compelling person ever to live, and I think that was the case because he *was* the good news as much as he *spoke* good news. He *spoke* of tenderness and then *showed* tenderness. When he spoke of wrath, fire blazed in his eyes and he turned over tables. He said God forgives sins, and he forgave sinners as they were in the act of killing him in the most mean-spirited, painful and humiliating way possible.

The Gospel is true whether we live it out or not. *Our* faithfulness is in question, not *God's* faithfulness (2 Timothy 2:11-13) or truth. But Jesus didn't tell us just to speak the truth; he told us to make disciples. If we are going to do what he told us, we have to ask more than just, "What is the truth?" We need to ask ourselves, *"What expression of this truth is the most persuasive?"* If we really love our city, we have to love them enough to tell the truth persuasively, and that usually means *graciously* and *sacrificially*.

At our church, most people become Christians because they come to the church and hear the preaching. However, almost no one decides to come to the church in order to hear the preaching. These people come because someone invited them, and usually because of something they observed in the life of the person who invited them. Sometimes they talk about the church's "buzz" in the community. But they are usually not talking about our Sunday services, though they're okay. They are talking about the church's effect on our people and their joy in it. These visitors have met people whom they admire, and then they found out that these people are Christians who go to our church.

THE UNSPOKEN FEAR

Every non-Christian who is thinking about faith wonders on some level what they would look like as a Christian. They are not looking for someone to clone, but they are looking for a picture they don't hate. They are looking for someone who does not embody all their objections to Christianity.

For some, the issue is coolness. They want to know they will not suddenly crave boring music or bad art if they follow Christ, or they want to know there won't be neckties or big hair involved. But that is not the heart of the issue. People can get over style-based and other shallow objections if they see a life of real beauty and nobility. They can overlook many quirks and oddities if they see at the center of our character a real renewed heart that loves God by loving other people. They will even drink bad, cheap coffee if they find themselves doing it with people whose faith makes them embrace sacrifice to change the world, to save lives and to save souls.

This is really the heart of *Blueprint* and the vision of High Point Church. It is the idea that the Gospel does not need to be anything other than what it is to connect us, grow us, and teach us to serve our earthly city in a way that will persuade many to join the eternal city.

Blueprint is not a church growth model. It is just the simple notion that the Gospel is relevant because it is a gospel; it is true and powerful saving news. *Blueprint* is the conviction that, for most people, Christianity "has not been tried and found wanting. It has been found difficult and left untried."[1] It is the idea that real holiness is the most attractive thing in the world, and that willing sacrifice motivated and empowered by the Spirit of Christ in us is the most compelling fulcrum of change in the human experience, both for the Church and for the city.

We have come to you with a simple but profound notion that we do not need to live the lies. We do not need to be typical modern Americans lightly seasoned with Christianity. Christ has made us into a new humanity, and we can wear our culture like clothes rather than mistaking our culture for our substance, and it is precisely this heavenly mindedness that has the potential to make some earthly good of us. It is precisely the primary place of our new citizenship that will give us the freedom to become great citizens of our earthly country. This kind of renewal is the only Christian kind that I know with certainty is really Christian. It is the only basket worthy of all our eggs, and it is the only way that can only fail by not being tried.

So like all short seasons of interest, you must decide what to do with this message when you put down this little book. Will it be for you the end of a stone's throw or the beginning of an avalanche? What will you carry with you when you drop these pages? Whatever else you take away, I'm praying that you will know God and connect with others a little more than you have. I hope you will diligently seek a deeper understanding of the Gospel and knowledge of the Bible and the God who speaks through it. I hope you will see how service transforms you while you pour yourself out to reach the city where God has planted you. God bless you, and thanks for doing this with us.

---

1   G.K. Chesterton, *What's Wrong with the World* (1910), (London: Catholic Way Publishing, 2013), 23.

APPENDIX 1
THE FIVE PURPOSES OF SMALL GROUPS

Small groups at High Point Church have five purposes:

1. Community and spiritual friendship

2. Study and spiritual discussion

3. Substantive prayer

4. Support missions

5. Serve others

COMMUNITY AND SPIRITUAL FRIENDSHIP

There is friendship, there is friendship with Christians and then there is spiritual friendship. Christian community is built on spiritual friendships. A spiritual friendship is one in which our spiritual identity is the issue in the friendship. You can have a friendship with a Christian in which you rarely talk about Jesus. Though that's technically a Christian friendship, it's not necessarily a spiritual friendship. In small groups, we are building a community of people who have relationships with each other in which Jesus is the issue. It is a community of spiritual friendships.

Now, to be clear, spiritual friendships have all the characteristics of other kinds of friendships. A spiritual friendship just has an additional dynamic as its most foundational one.

STUDY AND SPIRITUAL DISCUSSION

Small group should have discussion times when we talk about the gospel and the Bible. Most High Point small groups follow the sermon series. They discuss the sermon and study the Bible passage on which the sermon was based. Studying the Bible and talking about the Gospel, especially with a bias for application, helps foster a community of spiritual friendship in the group. Discussing the sermon allows anybody to participate even if the only experience of Christian faith they have is attending church the previous Sunday.

Studies and discussions are not always going to be incredibly exciting. But as I always tell the congregation, if small group is boring, it's because you are boring. So long as the group has a decently healthy dynamic, and people want to grow in their understanding of the Gospel and knowledge of the Bible, you shouldn't have much trouble finding something to discuss.

SUBSTANTIVE PRAYER

Faith is something that needs to be exercised. Trust gets stronger when it's active. Prayer is how we vocalize what it is we're trusting God about. We say out loud that which we need from God and that for which we are thankful.

Yet prayer time in most small groups is a time of complaining or gossiping, or really *anything* but praying. Requests that are shared—the things we're trusting God for—aren't personal. We spend most of our time praying for the relative of a coworker. The prayer requests aren't in the room.

So we have **three guidelines for prayer requests** in High Point small groups:

1. **The request has to be in the room**. We will not pray for anyone who isn't in the room or isn't normally there during small group prayer times. If the prayer request is for another person, we either invoke this rule and disqualify it, or we pray for the person who is in the room who God can use to minister to that person or request.[1]

---

1   Example of something I've said, "We aren't going to pray for your co-worker who is getting a divorce because of our rule to keep prayer requests in the room. But we will pray for God to use you to care about her, comfort her and love her." Then I will pray for her request personally to insure both that: 1. She knows it is important to me and I'm not just being mean, and 2. That no one else subverts the discipline in applying the rule by praying for the co-worker during the prayer time.

2. **Pray bigger than the group.** How should we pray for our larger church and the gospel movement we are a part of?

3. **Ask: "What would Jesus' prayer request for me be?"** If Jesus was to share what his deepest desire for you is, what would he say? That's the thing you should be praying for and inviting others to pray for.

The only rule I have about *how* we pray is that **I ask people not to pray for more than 30 seconds at a time.** People's attention spans just can't track much longer than that if one person is praying a monologue. Pray plainly and directly to God in simple language, then stop and let someone else pray. You can always pray again after some other people have gone. Bouncing around helps keep everybody engaged because every new person who prays resets the group's attention span. Also, the shorter and plainer you pray, the more new people will think, "Well, I can do *that*," and they'll pray out loud.

It is the small group leader's job to teach these rules from the very first meeting. They need to be strictly enforced and constantly restated. I find it takes about seven or eight meetings of restating these rules before they really start to happen on their own, and you usually have to disqualify two or three prayer requests before people really start thinking them through according to the rules.

If you do this, though, it can drastically change the spirit and practice of prayer in your small group for the better.

SUPPORT MISSIONS

Christian faith has a global mandate. Jesus said we're supposed to make disciples of all nations, yet it can be very difficult to get everybody in the church involved in this. Most churches just have a few people who are "really into missions," who contribute a certain percentage of the church's budget.

Yet the global mandate is for the whole church, and all of us have a contribution to make. Just as important, doing the work of supporting missions creates the vital connection we need for learning to care about the world and God's work in it. This is why we connect every small group with a missionary or missions organization and challenge them to find a way to support and encourage these people. We don't tell groups they should collect money. Individuals in the group are welcome to support the missionary, and the church as a whole supports missionaries.

The task of the small group is more relational. Being a missionary in a foreign nation can be very difficult. How can this group, in fairly simple and human ways, support and encourage these missionaries? Care packages? Prayer? Letters? For every group it will be different, but for every group it should be something. Personal contact and emotional support can make a huge difference.

SERVE OTHERS

The term we use for this is "organized service." We do that to distinguish between serving one of the church's ministries inside the church and serving something in the city outside the church. Hopefully every Christian is making a contribution through some church ministry, but our goal through small groups is to deploy groups of Christians to serve in the city.

Sometimes the service is still in Christian contexts. But whether it is with Christian ministries in the city, part of larger church initiatives to reach out or with organizations or people that are not connected with the church, the goal is to serve someone who is not us. The goal is for the church to serve the non-church.

We train small group leaders to make this happen at least quarterly. Sometimes it's done instead of the normal small group meeting so that it doesn't require an additional time commitment. But whatever the task and whatever the schedule, it needs to be done.

Service projects help all of the other small group components come together as well. Moving outside our church helps us have a more missional attitude about our city. It often starts relationships or connects us with something we want to pray for. Service experiences are memorable and tend to build spiritual friendships better than normal meetings. They also allow us to live out the bias for application we talk about in our study times.

All of the five purposes are connected. They are all important. They help us as a church to connect with God and others and grow in our understanding of the gospel and knowledge of the Bible, while serving the city and reaching the world. So if you're not in a group, get in one. If you are in a group, help make the five purposes the clear and constant mission of your group.

APPENDIX 2
Why Baptism?

As we think about belonging to the universal and local church, it's important that we have a shared understanding of baptism. First, baptism is a public rite of initiation in which someone takes on the name of Jesus and publicly becomes his follower, acknowledging him as the one in whom she has put her trust. It is how we express our profession of faith in Jesus, and we do it by mode of immersion, essentially submerging the person underwater and bringing her back up again.

There are a few things that you should know about baptism. First, there's the starting question: Do you need to get baptized? Well, the answer is "Yes." Baptism happens as soon as possible after personal conversion in the New Testament. There is no such thing in the New Testament as an unbaptized Christian, and baptism is mentioned in numerous places. Even the Ethiopian eunuch in Acts 8 knows that he should be baptized immediately after believing in Jesus.

Second, baptism is simple. Baptism is not a complicated and drawn-out experience in which one needs to perform great feats. You do something that most Western people do most days: you get wet. Baptism is a fairly straightforward and simple test of our sincerity in conversion. When we are converted, we say that we trust in Jesus for our salvation, and we have become his followers. Baptism is simply the recognition of this by getting dunked underwater. It's not exactly hard. It's not expensive. It's not an act only for "super Christians." It's just a recognition of something we say we've already done. It is a very simple way to show that you mean what you say, that you really do believe in and follow Jesus now.

Third, although baptism is simple, what it represents is still profound. Scripture teaches that it represents cleansing, death and resurrection. It symbolizes the fact that we are washed and made morally clean by the death and resurrection of Jesus applied to us. Baptism also symbolizes dying to sin and being raised in new life in Christ so that we belong to God and seek to obey him in everything (Colossians 2:12, Romans 6:4). In addition to symbolizing salvation, baptism designates someone as belonging to Jesus (that's why we say people are baptized "in his name") and to the universal Church (Ephesians 4:5).

Fourth, you need a ritual. Identity is partly connected to memory. You define who you are today in large part based on what you remember and on the interpretation of your memories. Committing to Jesus mentally and even saying that you believe in him are both things that can be corrupted in our memory over time. We start to ask ourselves: "Do I *really* believe? How *sincere* was I? Did I say it right or think the right things?"

Rituals and ordinances (things God has directed us to do to help us remember) are designed to make objective something that subjective memory and imagination can corrupt. The marriage ceremony is meant to demonstrate that the family-making covenant is objective and not subject to the whims of how "in love" you feel. Communion or "the Lord's Supper," the time when we eat bread and drink wine together to celebrate the broken body and blood of Jesus, shed to save us from our sins, is meant to be objective. No matter how internally confused we are about what good or bad Christians we are, Jesus still died for us. In taking communion, we proclaim that we believe it, that Jesus saves us through simple faith and that he will return.

Similarly, baptism marks out very specifically when we have become followers of Jesus. It marks when we formally put ourselves in a community, take on Jesus' name as our Savior and leader, and recognize that only Christ cleanses us, remakes us and ultimately raises us from the dead. We need that moment objectively marked out for us. We need to pledge in good faith and a clear conscience to Christ and his church that we are his. God believes it is necessary and important that we do this.

So if you have believed in Jesus, but you haven't been baptized on your own profession of faith, then it's time to step up and do it. It's time to publicly label yourself as belonging to Jesus. It's time to officially and formally declare to the other people in Christ's Church that you are their brother or sister, and that you want to be treated as such. It is important that you revel in and enjoy the fact that Christ has cleansed you from your sins, put to death your old life and given you a new one, and will ultimately raise you from the dead.

Jesus demonstrated his love for us by being humiliated and tortured in an unjust execution. His first commandment to us is that we allow ourselves to be submerged in a harmless liquid to show that we belong to him, so that his Church can celebrate over us the same way he does over every person who comes to repentance and trust. We can do this. If you haven't done this yet, and you believe, then it's your turn.

APPENDIX 3
Why Church Membership?

One of the questions that might come to mind again after reading about the church as a place of family, fellowship and community is "Should I rethink church membership?" Are you a member of your church? Why or why not?

Most people who resist church membership either don't think membership is biblical, or they don't think it's important. Yet church membership is what separates those who consume religious goods and services at a church from those who consider it their family, body and source of shepherding.

IS IT BIBLICAL?

The phrase "church membership" is not found anywhere in the Bible.[1] And yet, in a number of passages, it seems clear that people know who is on the *inside* and *outside* of the church. In Matthew 18:15-17, it says that if a brother refuses church discipline, the ultimate act of discipline is that he would be put out of the church. The whole passage assumes we know who is on the inside and who is on the outside.[2]

In 1 Corinthians 5:12-13 Paul explicitly tells them that they must judge those "inside the church," and they should let God judge those outside. He essentially says, "Judging those on the outside isn't any of your business. But judging those inside is your business." That is, the church was responsible for the accountability of those who were inside it though they could not control the behavior of those outside the church. Again, this assumes that we know who belongs

---

1   Neither are Trinity, substitutionary atonement or a number of other thoroughly biblical concepts.

2   See also Acts 5:12-13.

and who doesn't, who is on the inside and who is on the outside. You know who is in your family. Paul adds to this in 2 Corinthians 2:6 (probably referencing the same person in need of discipline earlier), saying that the punishment of the majority is enough, meaning the discipline of the majority of the church membership on this person who openly sinned.

In both Matthew's gospel and the letter to the Ephesians, it is assumed that the Church established by Jesus is a public, earthly institution that is marked out, affirmed and overseen by those who profess to believe in him.[3]

In Hebrews 13:17 and 1 Thessalonians 5:12-13, people are commanded to submit to the leadership of the church. Relationships of authority and shepherding both presume knowing who is inside and who is outside the fold. Who is under authority? Who are the people under the shepherds' care? In these cases and others, it is clear that a number of Christian commands require knowing who is on the inside and who is on the outside of the church. The distinction might not be called "church membership" in these texts, but it is exactly what we mean by church membership today.

IS IT PRACTICAL?

At what point should we consider someone part of the church? Many of these passages refer to submission to leadership and accepting discipline. Should we expect an anonymous attender to submit to the authority of the church's spiritual leaders? At what point is a regular attender supposed to do this? After one month? Three months? Four years?

With church membership, the answer is this: when they voluntarily choose to be part of the spiritual family and accept its responsibilities and benefits publicly. Formal church membership is an extremely practical and necessary

3   9Marks, "According to Scripture, why should every Christian join a church?" *Answers for Pastors*, 9Marks, http://www.9marks.org/answers/according-scripture-why-should-every-christian-join-church (accessed 15 Jul. 2014).

category in order to be the church as Jesus told us to function—with accountability, submission to leadership and mutual commitment.

That is not to say you can't be a real contributor to a church without being a member, but becoming a formal member displays to everyone an internal commitment and a sense of ownership. It is a shared pledge between you and the other people in the church. By membership, we tell others that they can depend on us. It changes the relationship from a business transaction to a family relationship.

Both business and family relationships have their place in human society. Even in churches, we will all have a period of "pre-commitment," whether our decision is about committing ourselves to Christ or about committing to a particular local church. But even this period of pre-commitment is *supported* by membership because membership makes the difference between these two relationships clear. It makes it so we know who is considering Christ or "checking out" the church and who is reliably part of this spiritual family. It allows people to check out Christian life and community before committing to the full responsibilities and discipline of real family. Yet, it also communicates to them that a deeper level of belonging exists. It allows them to be an insider or an outsider without confusing them or us about where anyone stands.

IS IT TOO RESTRICTIVE?

It's not uncommon, especially among younger Christians, for people to ask me, "What's wrong with being part of two or more churches? Why do I need to be committed to one church?" My answer is something like this: I wouldn't say it's wrong to be involved in some things at other churches. But there are two main things to consider in this situation. First, can any of these churches count on you to be a contributor, or can they only count on you to be a consumer? Secondly, where is your spiritual shepherd who can correct you, criticize you and get in your face when you really need it? Where is the spiritual leadership to which you actually submit (submission not being a consumeristic category)?

PASTORAL NECESSITY

Church membership is not only biblical and practical, but it is also pastorally necessary. Scripture commands that the local church be led by people called elders, overseers or pastors who are in specific authority. As elders, they are appointed because of their experience and exemplary life. As overseers, they have the authority to do the work of leading and ruling. And as pastors,[4] they have the task and role of providing for and protecting Christ's sheep.

When we become church members, we put ourselves under the authority and responsibility of the church's shepherds. Caring for us becomes part of their responsibility, and membership is the practical and public invitation we issue for them to care for us in encouragement, leadership and discipline. It is how we convey that we will follow them in our shared work for Christ. We invite them to confront us when we need it for our good, even if it feels like meddling. We show them where we are in relation to Christ's authority. They can come to see our attitudes and maturity because they can know quite a lot about our internal and spiritual relationship to Christ by observing our formal and physical relationship to the local church.

PROMOTION AND HORIZONTAL COMMITMENT

There are two important considerations for those who aren't elders. In a growing and thriving church, pastors and elders have to appoint numerous people to positions of leadership. Churches need various kinds of "under shepherds." By becoming a member, you signal to the church's leadership that you understand the relationship of commitment and authority necessary to be trusted with such a position. Positions of leadership require the stability of commitment,

---

4   The word "pastor" comes from the old French word *pastur* meaning, "herdsman, shepherd," the one who takes the flock out to pasture. Since about 1872, churches have used this word for a particular position inside the church. But in the Bible, it is used synonymously with elders and overseers (traditionally translated "bishops").

and the humility appropriate to one who is under authority. That is why many churches require church membership for teachers, deacons, ministry leaders and many other leadership positions.

Secondly, it matters to the people serving right beside you. Your commitment has a wider effect than you might think. Everyone around you is consciously or subconsciously taking in signals about how much they can count on you. What you show others about your level of commitment either raises their morale or diminishes it. When you become a member, you say, "You can count on me. I'm not just here until I find a better church. This is my church, and I'm here to make it better."

YOUR INVITATION

I was in my 20s, maybe eight years into my walk with Christ, before I joined the church. I'm from a generation that doesn't join anything. Disestablishment generations don't like established authorities and institutions, but society is bound together by establishments and institutions. It is through covenants and confessions that we are bound together in community, fellowship and friendship. When we commit to common missions and purposes, we can be led and can know when to follow. This was all difficult for me to accept, but the Bible slowly wore me down.

It was ultimately the reason I became a pastor. No institution is as great as its ideals, the Church least of all, since its ideals are so great. Yet when I accepted that Christ commanded his Church be instituted, I had to accept his institution. This meant that if I didn't like it, I had to rebuild and reform it, not reject it. And the only way this has ever been done is by committing to the universal Church by becoming more embedded in the actual local church. We learn to love the Church as Christ does, even when she fails to live up to her calling. We must become unapologetically part of a real, material, local and concrete spiritual family. We give our blood, sweat, passion and tears to that institution for the sake of those people and for the glory of the one to whom they belong.

Perhaps the name isn't exciting enough. Perhaps calling this "church membership" is a little like calling skydiving "altitude readjustment." But whatever the marketing, the meaning should confront us. And by confronting us, it invites us. What will you do?

APPENDIX 4

You Must Rest:
Sabbath in Sorting Everything Out

How hard does God want you to work for him or for anyone? Does God want to burn you out at both ends? Does he want to be a slave driver to others? Well, that's not as simple a question as one might think. On one hand, Paul can call himself the slave of Christ, a man who was always in want. He was cold, hungry, shipwrecked, beaten and imprisoned for the Gospel. Difficulty, persecution and withering exertion of will and body seemed to always follow him. Living as a Christian is a hard, honest day's work. But there is a special kind of sleep that follows real, purposeful labor. It is part of a rhythm of work and rest that isn't oppressive. There is a difference between work and slavery just as there is between slumber and sloth.

From the beginning, God has claimed that the objective difference between a workman and a workaholic is the ability to rest. If you apply the call to connecting, growing and serving in a way that doesn't just *stretch* you, but actually *thins* you, then you may be missing the important principle of rest called Sabbath.[1] It is the saving command given in love both to the unbelieving workaholic and to the pious workaholic. It is for both the man seeking to be his own savior and the one trying to be the savior of the world. The Sabbath restores the soul from both forms of madness and from the rest-banishing anxieties that accompany them.

FINDING RHYTHMS

In work, family and ministry, we have to find a rhythm of work and rest, exertion and relaxation, impartation and preparation. Even in physical labor, there is a pace at which we can work for a long time, but if we work just a little

---

1 Sabbath is another commanded ritual. We are commanded to rest, to remember God and to trust in his provision.

faster, we tire out almost immediately. Work has a sweet spot, and a huge part of it is finding the rhythms of work and rest, intensity and relaxation.

IDENTIFYING BURNOUT

It is your job to recognize and take action when you are burning out. A wise person knows the indicators of depletion and takes action before their emotional reserves get too low. If you're getting burned out, you need one of three things:

1. **A Rest:** You've been doing the right work for too long at too high a level of intensity. When you go back, build a better and more disciplined rhythm of work and rest.

2. **A Different Attitude:** You haven't worked too hard or too long, but the way you are thinking about your work causes you to be prematurely emotionally depleted. Because you don't like what you're doing or think it's valuable, you feel like you're wasting your time, not accomplishing anything or missing out on more important opportunities. You might need different work, but it's also likely you just need an attitude change. The most important work in the world is repetitive and mundane. Have a look at your thinking about work before you think too much about changing your work.

3. **A Different Work:** You may be getting burned out because you are not well-suited for the job you're trying to do. This is more likely the more specialized the work. Some work almost anyone can do. But certain kinds of work take special gifts, personal assets and expertise. The more a job or ministry requires, the higher the likelihood that you could end up poorly fitted to your job or ministry. Sometimes the only solution is figuring out what would fit you better.

CHOOSING MINISTRIES:
MAKING CONNECT-GROW-SERVE CHOICES

Some of the biblical pictures of being in Christ are: a body, a soldier, a worker, a manager, a family member, and so on. Almost every picture presumes either a relationship or a job in which one is morally obligated to make a contribution. A farmer's responsibility is to grow things. Every family member has a responsibility to the family. Every part of the body has its job to do. A manager is responsible for outcomes.

If you belong to Jesus, your heart should be driving you to want to make some kind of contribution in his family and for his purposes. That doesn't mean that you have to do any specific job within the local church on Sunday morning. Once you get your heart right about making a contribution, you can think through God's will regarding what you should do by asking the following questions.

QUESTIONS FOR FINDING GOD'S WILL

1. What does Scripture tell me to do and not to do? How does the Bible limit my options?

2. As I'm growing in Christ, what is in my heart and conscience to do?

3. What do godly people in my life advise?

4. Is there a real need and opportunity to do this?

5. Is the door open, or will it open with persistence?

6. What is my internal sense of God's leading telling me?

7. Does it fit my personal gifts, limitations, assets and resources? Does it fit me?

8. Is it intrinsically good, true and meaningful? Does it contribute something to others and the purposes of God, even if it's in very plain and simple ways?

I find that people who want to find God's will, who make a contribution and who are humble enough to listen to others will find good and meaningful labors. When these labors are put in their proper place with their proper rhythms in an attitude of service, people tend to thrive rather than burn out.

As you grow in Christ, what is in your heart and conscience to do?

What does Scripture forbid or enjoin?

What do godly people advise?

Is it a real need and opportunity?

FINDING GOD'S WILL(S)

Is it intrinsically good, true and meaningful?

Does it fit your personal gifts, limitations, assets and resources?

Is there an internal sense of God's leading?

Is the door open, or does it open with persistence?

APPENDIX 5
Answering Main Objections to Missionaries

READ ISAIAH 49:6 AND MATTHEW 28:18-20

WHAT GIVES US THE RIGHT?

The risen Christ has given his followers an absolute global missionary call. Yet we live in a country and a moment in which many count this as a terrible public sin against humanity. Those interested in sharing the message of Jesus locally (evangelism) and in global cross-cultural contexts (missions) have to face strenuous objections. We are either explicitly told or made to feel that we don't have the spiritual or moral authority to do this.

The objections are usually pluralistic and secular, focusing on four major accusations. They often sound something like this:

1. **Missions is colonialism and imperialism**, disrupting rich native cultures and treating them as inferiors. *Don't you see it's wrong to try to assimilate the diverse and rich cultures of the world and to try to make them just like you?*

2. Evangelism and missions are built on **arrogant and exclusivist assumptions** that "we're right and you're wrong." *How arrogant can you be to believe that your ideas are superior to others or your religion is better?*

3. Christianity is **destructive and violent**, as evidenced by its history. *Christianity has been a historic force of evil in the world, not of good. Why should the world want that exported to them?*

4. The world needs **science and pluralism** (which will end poverty and create harmony), not religion (which will just produce more fanaticism and violence). *What other nations really require is science, not religion. They need our*

advancements in politics, technology, economic development, education and healthcare. These are the real global solutions. These are the only truly universal and helpful resources. [1]

These arguments plant unnecessary doubt in the hearts of thousands—perhaps millions—of Christians. Yet all of them are overwhelmingly false either logically, historically or biblically.

THE COLONIALISM OBJECTION

Missions is often derided as a form of colonialism that hurts cultures and doesn't respect the humanity of the people in the receiving culture. Yet the story of real Western missionaries is very different. As I mentioned in the reading for Week 6: Day 4, John Paton was nearly killed more than once for standing up for the natives of the New Hebrides against Western traders. He was the lone voice against traders instigating native wars to make Western guns more valuable in trading and the practice of selling disease-infected goods among the tribes they didn't like.

Missionaries like Paton were often the only observers who were neither part of the native people, nor in agreement with the Western traders who might abuse them. His story, along with the other stories we mentioned, are only a small snapshot of the similar accounts recorded for us. The case of anyone, in any culture, standing against their own countrymen for the rights of "savage" natives is generally very rare, but it's not so rare among the Christian missionaries.

THE ARROGANCE AND EXCLUSIVISM OBJECTION

The accusation of arrogance and superiority immediately fails if we are offering the Gospel for others to freely accept or reject. It is up to the people of the nations of the world to decide whether they believe the Christian message

---

1 One of the ironic things about this attitude is that secularization is the most culturally disruptive and destructive force in the world. Cultures have the hardest time holding together not when they accept Christianity, but when they receive the rest of Westernization.

is true and worth believing.[2] This can only be discovered when beliefs clash, are discussed, lived out and exchanged. There is nothing arrogant or superior about offering someone something you believe is true and valuable. Arrogance and superiority enter in when you try to control people or shut them up. Ironically, that's exactly what this objection is designed to do to Christians.

THE VIOLENCE AND DESTRUCTION OBJECTION

Biblical Christian faith doesn't destroy cultures; it transforms them. Every culture Christianity has ever touched has remained culturally distinct from other Christians, while making changes informed by the Gospel and the Bible. Real Christian faith should amplify what's best in cultures, while awakening us to what's worst in our culture. It does that for our individual personal lives, and it does that within corporate cultural structures. It's true that sometimes this is disruptive, but many times it is a feature, not a bug.

For example, it was only in the Christian West that the institution of slavery was disrupted. Modern science was developed in the Christian West, and it disrupted life with new knowledge and technology and the increasing absence of starvation. The role of women was rethought on Christian grounds in the Christian West. In Christianized Rome, brutal executions were outlawed, gladiatorial games ended and Christians disrupted the cultural norm of infanticide and abandoning people afflicted by plague to die.

When Christian missionaries and British evangelicals went to India, the Hindu practice of *sati* (involuntarily burning of Hindu widows on their deceased husband's cremation pyre) was outlawed. In one account, when a Hindu priest complained that the British were interfering with Hindu customs and culture, Sir John Napier is said to have

---

2   Technically, withholding the Gospel would be just as arrogant as forcing it on people. In both cases we would be making a judgment about the worth of the Gospel for people rather than letting them make the decision themselves. Tyranny and pluralism share a kind of paternalistic superiority and arrogance. Offering something to a people to judge its worth for themselves bears neither.

responded:

> *"Be it so. This burning of widows is your custom; prepare the funeral pile. But my nation also has a custom. When men burn women alive we hang them, and confiscate all their property. My carpenters shall therefore erect gibbets on which to hang all concerned when the widow is consumed. Let us all act according to national customs."*[3]

This is intolerant, exclusivist and disruptive indeed. Many of these "disruptions" are precisely why people in these cultures became Christians by the thousands.

This is not to say that there have not been very many instances of harmful intolerance, harm and disruption caused by global missionaries and personal evangelists. Some were unforeseeable or unintended consequences, and some were certainly the product of wickedness and ignorance.

However, this was nothing like the norm, as is often pictured in secularist mythology. Further, these evils are much smaller in scale than the harm inflicted on the nations by secular, economic and governmental initiatives.[4] This is the third objection as to whether or not Christianity has been a force for good in the world.

We should all admit that there have been many wicked missionaries and many bad effects of missions that came from completely unintended consequences. Some objections are getting at things we need to pay attention to. Some ways of doing missions are more disruptive and more damaging to people than others. It is also true that the world has many temporal needs as well as eternal needs. Yet no missionary has ever said, "These people need Jesus, so they don't need clean water." The historical fact remains that Christian missionaries have been among the earliest and greatest forces

---

3   Sir Charles Napier, quoted in William Napier, *History of General Sir Charles Napier's Administration of Scinde* (London: Chapman and Hall, 1851), 35.

4   Most of the examples of brutality and exploitation came at the hands of the trading companies, not missionaries. Unintended consequences are part of globalization of any kind.

for global good throughout world history, both spiritually and materially.

THE SCIENCE AND POLITICS OBJECTION

You may often encounter the objection that the people of the world need our science, education and political philosophies to develop, not our religion, but this objection is circular in its logic. It must assume that the only important things in the world are empirical things, points of knowledge and social contracts. Very few humans have ever been so simplistic about the world. Most have recognized that whenever needs and conflicts exist outside of the human psyche, there is always a very great spiritual and moral battle within it. The consequence of this struggle affects everything that happens outside of people, including what they do with science, education and political philosophies.

It is also circular reasoning because it presumes that humans have no spiritual needs or problems. If that's true, then perhaps there really is no need for a spiritual provision or solution. But one must firmly establish that argument as sound before its consequence can be true, and not only is that not possible, but people making this objection rarely even acknowledge that it's the necessary starting point for their position.

This is precisely where the Bible rejects the assumption behind this objection. The Bible presumes everywhere that the biggest problem in the world—the biggest problem for every human and group of humans—is a spiritual problem. When we leave room for this reality, there is no room for this objection. People making this objection are rarely expected to defend their starting point, but they should because it is indefensible.

There is a problem in the human heart and spirit that our empirical sciences, social theories and political philosophies are incapable of controlling or curing. Christian faith is not only realistic about this disease, but it is the only "technology," theory or philosophy with the capacity for its cure.

It has always been true that the surrounding world has told Christ's followers that we don't have the authority to make disciples of Jesus. The objections are old, repetitive and predictable. Jesus anticipated all of them. This is why he told us that all of the authority in heaven and on Earth belong to him. Therefore, he has the right to tell us we have the authority to do this. Therefore, no one has the right to tell us we can't.

APPENDIX 6
The Discipline of Following

One of the things I tire of is the claim in movies and cartoons that we all have to have our own little dreams. Great dreams require many people. It is simply not possible for everyone to have their own particular dreams. What if Martin Luther King, Jr.'s dream was only his dream and not a dream shared by a great many people? It is not incumbent upon us morally, nor taught anywhere by the Savior, that we should all have our own little individual dreams that we have made up.

In John 15:15, Jesus says, "I no longer call you servants, because a servant does not know his master's business. Instead, I have called you friends, for everything that I learned from my Father I have made known to you." That is, Jesus came to fulfill the Father's dream, and he has chosen his disciples to complete that work. It is considered an unspeakable joy to be included in the privilege of following Jesus in this way. In order for great things to happen, the fact is that most of us are going to have to be followers most of the time.

We can't accomplish anything by all being leaders. That's why visions and dreams are a little different in that you *cast* a vision and you *have* a dream.

Leadership starts with a dream that can be shared as a vision. That is, a leader's dream must be a dream that could just as easily be someone else's dream. This is because a vision must be so compelling that many people will drop their lesser dreams because they love the vision more. They love it so much that they would rather be one among many working for the vision than have their personal dream alone.

This is why we, as Christ's people, cannot allow our sense of vision to be deeply affected by our individuality and our consumption of goods and services. There is a self-lessness to good dreams and great visions. These character-istics should be shared both by the leader sharing the vision and by all who commit themselves to it.

My point here is not to explain the full significance of the visions we might have for our country, family or church. My point is only that it is just as noble to commit oneself to a great vision as to come up with one. If any progress is to be made in the actualization of anyone's vision, we will need much more of the latter than the former.

THE GIFT OF THE COMMITTED FOLLOWER

The heart of almost any great story is its secondary characters. Although God could carry a story by himself, he has chosen not to. He has chosen to use countless humans throughout many cultures and in every generation. In every human endeavor, there is a group of followers who make the difference between a vision being realized and a vision going nowhere. The greatest gift any leader can receive is people who can lead who are also willing to follow. These are the people who may make the greatest difference be-cause this is the criteria for success that is most often miss-ing. There are many followers, and there are many people who imagine themselves to be point leaders. The question is always, will the leader-followers turn this into a movement? Will there be people with the ability to give orders who will take them? Will there be people who could run something who are willing to run part of something? Is there someone able to be a dictator who is willing to be a colleague?

One of the most important times in my life was when I was the second-place leader in an organization. At the first church where I pastored, I was a Teaching Pastor serving under a Senior Pastor. There were many days when I would rather have done things my way and even would have pre-ferred to work in a smaller organization in order to have the freedom to do whatever I wanted. The closer you are to a leader and the more capacity you have to lead yourself, the more obvious you think their feelings are, and the more human they tend to look.

And yet, looking back, I never could have accomplished alone what we accomplished together. Or more pointedly, I realized that if I became the point leader, I would need a me, someone with leadership capabilities who was willing to support the vision and build the movement without being in charge of it. If I wasn't willing to do that, why should God provide someone to do it for me? Serving as a second-chair leader-follower was one of the most important experiences of my life in preparing for point leadership. I learned that committed leader-followers were the difference between a wispy dream and a vision that can become a reality.

THE NOBILITY OF FOLLOWING

The nobility of following is almost completely lost in our present culture. People question all forms of hierarchy and authority. People naturally ask the question, "Why should I have to listen to anyone?" Yet following has its own nobility because it knows the hidden secrets of humility.

People who are willing to take orders and get to work get things done. People who have to have a say in every-thing tend to spend most of their time talking. Not only does everything have to be said, but everybody has to have their turn saying it. The nobility of following has two components:

1. Noble followers are keen judges of character and competence. They are good at discerning whether they should follow someone.

2. They know coordination and maximization of the time spent working are critical to achieving large accomplishments.

Noble followers don't follow blindly, but once they have discerned the trustworthiness of whomever they are follow-ing, obedience becomes a virtue of diligence. It creates an environment where people work to accomplish a worth-while vision, rather than constantly talking about what might be a vision that is worthwhile.

The virtue of following is built into the very concept of discipleship. We are first and foremost Christ's disciples, and as such, we emulate and follow each other in the structures he has instituted and commanded. Most churches do not have heavily hierarchical structures anymore. Yet accomplishment still requires leadership, and effective leadership always wields authority, whether formal or informal.

BEING A DREAMER

Be free of the idea that you have to have your own dream. You do not need your own dream. In fact, that misses the point of the whole idea of what a dream is—a spontaneous picture of a reality from which you know not where it comes. In some ways, a dream comes to you. You don't create it. A dream is something that comes upon you while you are pursuing something else. Most people's particular dreams happened while they were pursuing the truth and facing reality. Dreams are like originality or creativity; they hardly ever happen when you pursue them directly. They tend to happen when you pursue something else.

If you don't have a dream, try following a great vision and a trustworthy leader. If you do have a dream, see if anybody else finds it and you worth following. If not, you might want to go back to "following a great vision and a trustworthy leader." In any case, most of the greatest dreams come to those who are seeking the truth and attempting to do good. Or, to put it shortly, seek God himself and his kingdom, and all these other things will be added to you as well (Matthew 6:33; Luke 12:32).

The most important thing about dreams is not that you have your own but that you work for a worthwhile one, whether you are the dreamer of the dream, the speaker of the vision, the leader of the movement or the baggage handler of the company makes little difference.

APPENDIX 7-A
Applying Spiritual Friendships

READ JOHN 15:1-15

REAL COMPASSION REQUIRES RELATIONSHIP BETWEEN THE SERVER AND THE SERVED

Friendship is an odd category. It can be one of the most trite and undependable categories in the world. But it can also be one of the deepest and most fulfilling relationships in human life.

A while back, my wife and I were talking with a couple from our church named Dave and Kim. Kim was talking to Alexi (my wife) about the people she was planning to invite to a child's birthday party. But when she named one family, Dave spoke up and said, "Baby, don't invite those people. They aren't our friends!" To which his wife shot back, "What do you mean?! Of course they are our friends!" Dave's reply stuck with me, "No, a friend is someone you can count on when you need help, and those people aren't our friends."

Dave was not saying the people in question were not perfectly wonderful people, he was just saying they were not one of their people. They're not people they would gladly sacrifice for or who would gladly sacrifice for them. They are not people who would think that making a sacrifice for them was a privilege rather than an inconvenience.

I knew there was something I liked about Dave's definition of friendship, and then I came across it in the Bible. Friends (and I'm using the deeper sense of the word) are people who love each other and gladly sacrifice for each other. They are people who have no ulterior motives and are not trying to manage you. They seek the good of each other, and through that, they make each other's lives more joyful and happy. If you look closely, almost all of these things are in John 15 in the friendship between Jesus and his followers.

LOVE AND SACRIFICE:

Jesus said, "My command is this: Love each other as I have loved you. Greater love has no one than this, that he lay down his life for his friends" (John 15:12-13). Love is only believable when it is perceivable, and there is nothing that makes love more obvious than sacrifice. The more sacrifice we offer without prospect of repayment, the more we show the purity of our love. Jesus gave everything for his friends, and in dying he made it impossible for them to try to repay him. He set in motion a line of love that could never be a circle, and in doing so, he spread an ever-growing web of love across the planet. The disciples could not lay their lives down for Jesus literally, but only on Jesus' behalf for someone else to whom they would offer real friendship through love and sacrifice.

ULTERIOR MOTIVES AND MANAGING PEOPLE

Jesus goes onto say, "I no longer call you servants, because a servant does not know his master's business. Instead, I have called you friends, for everything that I learned from my Father I have made known to you" (John 15:15). Jesus is the one person who could rightly treat any man as a servant. But he and the Father chose that these followers would be friends, not servants. God knew that a friend would always be a better servant, and only a person willing to serve could be a real friend. God himself proved this unshakable fact.

The point here is that Jesus did not offer his friends a sales pitch. He did not flatter them or use them as networking contact points. In fact, in three verses, he will warn them that the world is going to hate their guts if they are his friends. Before it is over, he will tell them they will be persecuted, and most of them will be killed for living out this friendship.

Though this is not exactly warm and fuzzy, it shows one important thing: Jesus wasn't managing these guys. He just told them the truth and put the right to make a decision in their hands. The truth is the foundation of intimacy and an indispensable part of real friendship.

MAKE LIFE MORE JOYFUL

Up to this point, you might say, this is all very romantic and honorable, but it is also a bit depressing! But that is not at all how Jesus saw this friendship. Just before this he said, "I have told you this so that my joy may be in you and that your joy may be complete" (John 15:11).

Jesus knew that the message he brought and the relationship these followers had with him was able to fill them with a kind of joy that would only be increased on the hard road of obedience. Friendship brings joy, and this friendship brings perfect joy.

There is one little difference here that is not normal in most friendships: Jesus would not stick around for his followers to love him back. The love he gave them could only be returned through their love for each other. This is why love would have to look like obedience, and obedience would have to look like service.

Once we understand this dynamic, we can understand how John would later help people test and see if they were really converted. In 1 John 3:14, 16-17 he said:

> *We know that we have passed from death to life, because we love our brothers. Anyone who does not love remains in death…This is how we know what love is: Jesus Christ laid down his life for us. And we ought to lay down our lives for our brothers. If anyone has material possessions and sees his brother in need but has no pity on him, how can the love of God be in him?*

In this, we're given three important details about applying our friendship with Jesus. First, we become his friend by faith in him giving his life for us. Second, we must realize that we can only love him by loving our brothers and sisters and by serving others. Third, this is a practical and measurable matter not to be taken lightly. The example John uses is about a real physical need. If we saw such a need, how could we not care about it? That would be impossible for someone who loved and knew how practical love is. We can hardly expect sympathy for not thinking love is a practical thing. The Savior did the most practical thing possible: he saved our lives with his life.

When we let this practical sacrifice lead us to obey the Savior in serving others, we will remain in his love (John 15:9). The result of this, he promised, was that his joy would be in us so that our "joy may be complete."

APPENDIX 7-B
Applying Friendships To Those In Need

Once we've internalized the general teaching of Christian friendship and love, we must apply it to those whom we will serve who are in need. It is commonplace today that charitable care is delivered through institutions and professional experts. Individual, direct volunteering in care of the poor and dysfunctional is becoming much less common since the common man and woman are reckoned unqualified to work with the complex psychological, economic, biological and social factors that lead to poverty and dysfunction.

Not only is this presumptuous and unwarranted privileging of experts, it is a fantasy. Social scientists constantly tell us that close relationships within tight social structures are the real catalysts of change, and even the most well-intentioned and well-resourced government agencies will always be hard pressed to create these parameters. Yet friendship can.

This reality was known to an earlier generation of Christian Americans who treated social problems very differently than we do today. In Marvin Olasky's book *The Tragedy of American Compassion,* he discusses a 200-year conviction in all Judeo-Christian health organizations that care for the poor and dysfunctional must be direct and personal. It's not that they saw no place for experts. In fact, many experts were utilized in the care of the poor. Yet direct relationships between people motivated by charitable love and the actual people in need was greatly encouraged and carefully structured. Today, some people have proposed similar mentoring approaches, sometimes called "direct friendship models."[1]

---

1   One modern author advocating this is Ruby K. Payne. Ruby K. Payne, Philip E. DeVol and Terie Dreussi Smith, *Bridges out of Poverty: Strategies for Professionals and Communities* (Highlands, TX: aha! Process, Inc., 2001).

Olasky offered four reasons why direct relationships between the recipients of care and compassionate volunteers are so important.

1. **Invigorates generosity and compassion:** People who regularly work with the poor tend to be more invigorated in working with them. People talk about compassion and generosity more, and knowledge spreads more readily.

2. **Involves rather than excludes donors:** When large agencies (particularly government-run ones) do the work without volunteers, there is a separation between the workers and the donors which tends to lead to less donations. It has been observed more than once that when government programs get involved in a social problem, private charitable funds tend to dry up.

3. **Creates intra-class empathy:** Empathy is grown in relationships. Different classes have very different experiences, and people from other lifestyles do not understand them until they see those differences in action. This is true for both groups' perceptions of each other.

4. **Helps separate poverty and tragedy from indolence:** The only way to reasonably separate the deserving poor from the undeserving poor is by knowing each individual poor and needy person. Agencies can never sufficiently accomplish this. There is never enough money or time. Relationships are the most effective means of figuring out what is actually going on in any particular situation and what is needed for that person to improve.

The main thing we should recognize is that the Church does not have to be in competition with government organizations, whether we agree with their scope or not. A relationship of teamwork will have to be worked out between what we do through our different levels of government and what we can do personally and through local churches.

The main thing to remember is that friendship is the most transformative thing we have to offer. Sacrificially serving others over the long-term in very specific areas of need has a greater likelihood of producing change in the context of poverty and dysfunction than any other method we have yet concocted. Direct relationships have many positive unintended consequences, while we have learned the hard way that disconnected approaches have many negative unintended consequences.

Compassion, when rightly done, has to be personal, and by personal I mean primarily *in person*. When this is done, both parties are more often transformed for the better. When this one criteria is neglected, much is lost that could have been gained.

APPENDIX 8
Purity With Presence

I have written you in my letter not to associate with sexually immoral people, not at all meaning the people of this world who are immoral, or the greedy and swindlers, or idolaters. In that case you would have to leave this world. But now I am writing you that you must not associate with anyone who calls himself a brother but is sexually immoral or greedy, an idolater or a slanderer, a drunkard or a swindler. With such a man do not even eat.

1 Corinthians 5:9-11

Hidden within this morally disturbing passage is a very important idea about how we live as the people of God in the world. Paul is addressing a church with lots of problems in one of the most sexually immoral cities in the ancient world. But Paul is not rebuking the city; he is rebuking the church. He is not upset that the church has not judged the city for its immorality. He is upset that they have been proud to accommodate such immorality from a confessing believer within their church. He is very clear: throw this guy out of the fellowship. Exert what is called "church discipline" on him, and see if it leads him to repentance. The move is both for his good and for the health of the church.

Now, some people have gotten the idea from this passage that the church should major in judging people and separating itself from everyone who is publicly sinful. Nothing could be further from the truth. Paul is clearly making the opposite point. In verses 9-10, Paul makes an extremely important distinction. What makes all the difference is whether or not the person in question calls himself a Christian and is part of the public church.

He forbids associating with an immoral person only if that person "calls himself a brother." That is, if he or she claims to belong to Jesus. Paul explicitly says he is "not at all meaning the people of this world." That is, people who are not confessing or baptized believers. He says it is God's business to judge the world, but we must sometimes discipline those in the church (1 Corinthians 5:12).

Now what is the point of all this unpleasantness? If it is God's business to judge the world, why wouldn't it be just as much his business to judge the Church too? Why must this be done by us?

The reason is bound up with the very nature of what the Church is. The Church is the community of the Gospel. As such, it is God's main sign to the unbelieving world of his truth, love, faithfulness, grace, willingness to sacrifice and reconcile, and every other facet of his revealed character. Therefore, the Church must be a pure counter-culture that can effectively display the Gospel. She cannot allow herself to be corrupted and made like the world because then she cannot be a sign to the world. Her whole mission rests on this clear identity.

Yet, the Church is not to purify the world through separation but by invitation. The Church cannot be a sign within the unbelieving world while simultaneously being separated from it. To be separate from the world would defeat the whole purpose of the Church. A sign must be visible, and a witness must be audible.

So however uncomfortable the practice of this passage makes us, the dual identity of the Church is clearly taught: the Church's mission is to be a pure counter-culture living as a hopeful sign within unbelieving communities. We must be deeply imbedded within the culture, yet radically different from it, and we can only accomplish this together.

APPENDIX 9
Gospel Confusions:
Self-Salvation Alternatives

When trying to understand what the Gospel is with clarity, sometimes it's helpful to understand what the Gospel is not. The Gospel is trusting in Christ and Christ alone as God's provision for our salvation. Jesus is the God and provider that we look to, and his death and resurrection is the means by which we are saved. Counterfeit gods will redefine what salvation is, who or what can provide for us, and what means we use to seek it.

Below is a list of what the Gospel is not. Having a clear sense of what the Gospel is not helps us clarify through differentiation what the biblical Gospel of Jesus is. This will help us see counterfeits, know the truth, trust God and live according to the Spirit.

1. **Irreligion:** Religion and anything that sounds like it isn't important.

2. **Profligate Hedonism:** Complete abandonment to pleasure seeking and pain avoidance. You only live once (YOLO), and the candle burned on both ends burns brightest. Now is the only moment there is, and we only have today. Live for the moment with a YOLO mentality. Think of the younger brother in Luke 15. This philosophy has been described with different adjectives in different ages and spheres of society: Bohemian when connected to the arts; Apollonian when blindly seeking dreams; Academic Hedonism when aimed toward reason and the sublime; and Dionysian when seeking sensuality and immediate experience.

3. **Epicurean Hedonism:** Pleasure seeking that takes the long view on happiness. There is a delicate relationship between taking pleasure and being smart in

maximizing pleasure for the long term.

4. **Moral Therapeutic Deism:** God appreciates that I'm a good person (moral), he's not overly involved in my life (deism) and he's there to basically make my life nice and me happy (therapeutic). This is the view of many Americans who identify themselves as Christians.

5. **Behavior Modification:** Faith can make my life more effective, and by applying religion, I can make myself a better person. This is my goal, and by using wisdom, spiritual techniques and discipline, I can achieve it.

6. **Moralism:** I'm a good, worthwhile person, and I deserve salvation because I do certain things.

   a. **Disestablished Moralism:** I'm awesome because I don't believe in any of that establishment, straight-laced nonsense. I'm good because I don't care about other people's conceptions of goodness or their expectations.

   b. **Religious Moralism:** I do the main things my religion requires, so I'm a good person. I may not live up to the point of the commands, but I do what's commanded.

   c. **Relative Moralism:** I'm better than most, so I should be okay. It would be unreasonable for God to be upset with me given that I'm not as bad as a lot of people.

   d. **Selective Moralism:** Because I do X, Y and Z, I'm officially a good person. The most important thing is X, and I do X consistently. I may have some failings, but at least I do X. This is what the person considers to be the most important thing for a person to be decent and worthwhile. It could be common sense, hard work, good education, self-sufficiency, avoiding irresponsible sexual choices, etc.

   e. **Communitarian Moralism:** Good people are Y, and I'm a Y, so I'm good. This appears in group memberships that rally around a particular ideology, whether it's political Liberalism, Progressivism, Conservatism, Libertarianism, vegetarianism, pro-gay/anti-gay rights activism, environmentalism, capitalism, etc.

f. **Consumption Moralism:** We mistake the often true good achieved by investing in "socially conscious" goods and services (green companies, charitable companies, non-establishment companies, etc.) as the ultimate good, believing either consciously or subconsciously that we can save our world from the bleak trajectory we fear or at least save ourselves from culpability in it.

All of these are forms of self-salvation. All of these are ways in which we can take control and provide for ourselves. All of these are based on some kind of idolatry and rejection of what God has explicitly said and specifically done. When we give our devotion to a different god in order to get a life that we want (redefined "salvation"), we move away from the Gospel of God's free gift of salvation to some form of self-salvation. If we do that, we are no longer believing the Gospel. We have rejected the message about Jesus, and we have lost our connection to the head in the saving recognition that God saves freely by his own grace and saves us by his own power.

Spend time trying to understand these counterfeit gods. Then try to identify them in your own thinking and feeling. Finally, when you identify them in your daily life, be quick to reject them and turn your heart to trusting in Christ and the Gospel.

APPENDIX 10
The Mission of the Church and a Christian

One of the things we say around here is that "every Christian should be part of a local church that knows that it's part of something bigger." That means that you can't be part of the larger church without being part of the smaller church. To concretely be part of the universal church you have to be part of a real, actual, concrete local church with real people. Unfortunately, there are many local churches that act as though they are in and of themselves. They don't seem to know that they are part of something a lot bigger.

I found that the two categories—the universal church and the local church—aren't enough to understand how we are part of something bigger. There are at least six manifestations of the church that we can talk about.[1]:

1. **The Cultural Church:** How the culture on the outside sees the church. This is what we look like to what the Bible calls "the world," or the nonbelieving culture that doesn't submit themselves to Christ's rule. Sometimes they see things we can't see, and sometimes they believe stereotypes about Christians that are false.

2. **The Local Church:** A concrete body of people who meet together as a spiritual family, under biblical leadership, to worship God, have fellowship with each other, celebrate the ordinances, hear the word of God and lovingly embrace church discipline.

---

1   A more complete discussion would include the "global church," which is all the Christians in every culture, ethnicity and language group that are presently alive in our time. This differs from the universal church since the universal church is not only the entire global church, but the entire global church at all times, past present and future.

3. **The Denominational Church:** A larger group of churches connected by a tradition or particular set of beliefs. Denominations are one way people of similar tradition, doctrine and understanding can team up and accomplish more together.

4. **The Regional Church:** The church connected by local geography. Any region has a number of Gospel believing churches of different denominations, leadership styles and idioms of ministry. Although they may not share some important convictions, they share a wider witness to the city as a whole. The regional church is Christ's witness to a region. They should work together to maximize the quality of that witness.

5. **The Structural Church:** Often churches that do ministry in a certain kind of way have more in common than churches in a region or even in a denomination. Often this equates with church size. The realities of doing church with 1500 people creates a system of dynamics, problems and needed solutions that bring churches of similar size, model, governance and style together. These are often informal networks but some of the most vibrant networks.

6. **The Universal Church:** The complete group of all believers mystically united through faith in Christ from every nation, time, language, ethnicity, gender and every other human distinction that exists. It is everyone who belongs to the people of God from every place and every time. They are one family together, united in Christ, and will be the one church forever.

Understanding these distinctions will help you understand if your church knows that it's part of something bigger. It will also help you understand some of the actions the church is taking. For example, your church may be supporting a church plant of a group that doesn't believe everything you believe. Why would it do that? It may be because your church belongs to the same structural church or regional church and your church's leadership believes that strengthening that church is important for the body of

Christ within that structure or region.

You may wonder why your church will work with another church in certain things but not in others. For example, it may partner with the church to advocate for religious freedom or to fund a food pantry. But it may not want to share in joint worship services or a regional youth ministry. This may be because while the religious freedom in food pantry partnerships strengthens the regional church's witness, the churches' convictions aren't similar enough to collaborate for joint worship or the spiritual formation of young people. Sometimes churches will work more closely with churches outside their denomination than with churches inside of it. This may be because they feel a closer affinity with other churches in their structural church or regional church.

When all things are said and done, the point of each local church is to take the number of people who have a view of the cultural church that is negative and help them become part of the universal church. We do this by being a local church that knows it's part of something bigger. We're part of the denominational church that shares our history and theological convictions most closely. We're part of a regional church with whom we collaborate to maximize the quality of our witness for Christ in our geographical area. We are part of the structural church, helping to build other churches like ours in size, style and tactics.

This can only happen when local churches recognize they are part of something bigger. They have to believe it as a deep conviction. They have to believe that participating in the universal church means working with the real people in the structural church, regional church and denominational church. Then they have to act out those convictions and beliefs.

Churches that understand the multiple manifestations of the church are churches that plant new churches. They engage in global, cross-cultural and cross-linguistic church planting. They care about whether the churches that serve other ethnicities are strong, while seeking to welcome all ethnicities in their own church. They encourage churches that believe all of their theological convictions, but they also encourage and serve Gospel believing and theologically orthodox churches that differ in emphases, tactics, style and ways of applying the Gospel.

The irony of seeing the church this way is that you can become more committed to the regional, structural, denominational, universal, global and cultural church by becoming more committed to a particular local church. There is something disingenuous about insisting that the universal church is very important to you and that is why you are not deeply committed to a particular local church. Instead, be deeply committed to a local church that knows it's part of something bigger. Understand the different manifestations of the church and how that affects the way your church seeks to be part of something larger. Encourage your church to be generous outside of its walls, not just to the community, but to other churches serving the community.

> It takes the whole church to deeply affect the way the whole culture sees her and sees the Gospel through her.

This is important not just because unity is important. It is important not just because it accepts the reality that we are ultimately one universal church. It is also important because the unbelieving world cannot change their mind about us in mass through one church being "different than all those other churches." There are a lot of churches and church plants out there that are "a different kind of church" or are for "people who don't like church." I know what these churches are trying to do and on some level I appreciate it. But it takes the whole church to deeply affect the way the whole culture sees her and sees the Gospel through her. Regional revival always comes through the regional church, and it tends to grow out of interchurch cooperation.

If a few churches live these convictions out with a deep passion, they are contagious. As the number of churches that embrace a larger vision grows, the unity that precedes revival grows with it. This starts with you:

1. Be part of a church that knows it's part of something bigger.

2. Insist your church doesn't spend all its money on you or itself.

3. Insist your church supports its "competitors" (others in the regional church).

4. Insist your church gives a healthy amount to global missions.

5. Insist your church be involved in church planting, even within your own region.

The whole kingdom of God functions on the principle of holy grace. Generosity is one of God's core values. When the church freely gives what it has freely received it comes into line not just with God's power, but his own intention, ethics, purposes and desires. There is no telling what redemptive power he might unleash upon us for the good of our churches, and more importantly, for the redemption of all people.

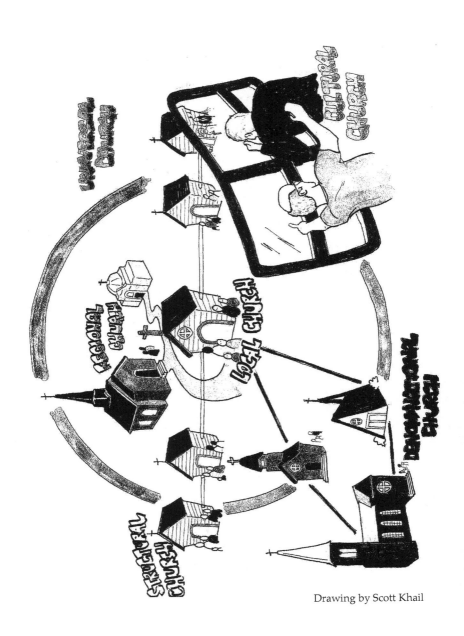

Drawing by Scott Khail

APPENDIX 11

The Gospel in Pictures

GOD
He always was, is and will be the God of the universe. Creator of all things.

US
God created humans out of love, with a purpose, and in his own image.

AUTONOMOUS & RESPONSIBLE
God made us able to make our own choices, and we used that capacity to go our own way.

SIN
This rebellion and rejection of God and his purpose is called "sin." It has its own consequences, effects and penalties.

DEBT OWED
Under sin we are dominated, enslaved, deluded and condemned.

THE SOLUTION
God initiated a plan of redemption by coming himself in the person of his Son, the man Jesus Christ.

THE SACRIFICE
In the cross, Jesus absorbed the wrath of God against us in order to set us right with God.

THE RESURRECTION
Christ's resurrection proves his identity as God and his success in defeating sin and death.

CONVERSION
The only condition of Christ's redemption is repentant faith. We have to admit that we are wrong and put our trust in Christ to set us right with God.

A NEW HEART
In Christ we experience the miracle of regeneration. He supernaturally remakes spiritual life in you.

JUSTIFIED
In Christ we are morally accepted according to Christ's goodness, since Christ was condemned morally according to our sinfulness.

FREEDOM & SANCTIFICATION
In Christ you are free from sin's domination and enslavement. You no longer have to sin. You can live a life of goodness and beauty.

HOLY SPIRIT
In Christ, the person of the Holy Spirit lives in and with you. You are not alone.

PART OF THE KINGDOM
In Christ, by belonging to God, you belong to something bigger: his creation, re-creation and redemption of all things. You have a new purpose.

ETERNITY
God's generosity knows no bounds. He promises us an eternity with him.

Made in the USA
Charleston, SC
13 January 2017